on track ...
Journey

every album, every song

Doug Thornton

sonicbondpublishing.com

Sonicbond Publishing Limited
www.sonicbondpublishing.co.uk
Email: info@sonicbondpublishing.co.uk

First Published in the United Kingdom 2025
First Published in the United States 2025

British Library Cataloguing in Publication Data:
A Catalogue record for this book is available from the British Library

Copyright Doug Thornton 2025

ISBN 978-1-78952-337-9

The right of Doug Thornton to be identified
as the author of this work has been asserted by him
in accordance with the Copyright, Designs and Patents Act 1988.
All rights reserved. No part of this publication may be reproduced, stored in a
retrieval system or transmitted in any form or by any means, electronic, mechanical,
photocopying, recording or otherwise, without prior permission in writing from
Sonicbond Publishing Limited

Typeset in ITC Garamond Std & ITC Avant Garde Gothic
Printed and bound in England

Graphic design and typesetting: Full Moon Media

on track ...
Journey

every album, every song

Doug Thornton

sonicbondpublishing.com

To Jocelyn, for telling me to stop talking
about it and write it already.

Acknowledgements

I could not write about 250 or so tracks without acknowledging the talented people who created them. Thank you to all the songwriters, performers, producers and engineers. Neal Schon, Jonathan Cain and Steve Perry have written the lion's share of these songs. My criticism of a guitar solo, synthesizer note, or lyric reflects more on my preferences than the quality work of these composers and musicians.

To all the Journey fans who keep their sites, blogs and video channels and who take to social media to post and talk about the band, thank you for inspiring me to write this book.

To readers Amber Goldman and Margot Stillings, thank you for your feedback and for helping me make this book better. Amber, I hope you come to appreciate the musical glory of 'Escape', and I don't hold it against you or anyone else for liking 'After Glow'. Of course, any mistakes within are mine and mine alone.

To Stephen Lambe for his patience and for publishing this book series. Special thank you to Dominic Sanderson for the developmental edits and for challenging me to make a better book.

My family have been very supportive and encouraging. Thanks to my daughters and sons and their spouses. Deecy, our Labrador Retriever, keeps me sane or at least in motion. Jocelyn, I'm feeling that way, too.

on track ...
Journey

Contents

Introduction	10
The Band Before 1975	12
Journey (1975)	14
Look Into The Future (1976)	19
Next (1977)	23
Infinity (1978)	28
Evolution (1979)	35
Departure (1980)	42
Dream, After Dream (1980)	48
Captured (1981)	52
Escape (1981)	58
Frontiers (1983)	67
Raised On Radio (1986)	76
Journey's Hiatus (1987-1995)	84
Trial By Fire (1996)	87
Arrival (2001)	94
Red 13 (2002)	101
Generations (2005)	104
Revelation (2008)	109
Eclipse (2011)	118
Solo Work, Relationships, Arrests And The Hall Of Fame (2011-2019)	124
Freedom (2022)	126
Compilations	134
Live Albums	139
Selected Films	148
Bibliography	149

Introduction

Bands with such longevity have complicated histories and Journey are no exception. The one constant through Journey's history is guitarist Neal Schon (rhymes with 'on'). He was the catalyst for manager Walter 'Herbie' Herbert to consider forming a band in the fertile San Francisco music scene. Schon has played guitar since he was a child, and after a successful two-album run as the second guitarist in Santana, Herbie wanted to create a band around the young prodigy.

Journey, despite the rich talent of its guitarist, would struggle for commercial success. Ultimately, Journey would be more identified with its lead singers, especially 'The Voice', Steve Perry. Fans usually organize Journey's history by the singers.

Gregg Rolie Era

From its founding in 1973 through the first three albums (*Journey*, *Look Into The Future* and *Next*), Gregg Rolie was the voice of Journey as he had been for Santana's biggest chart hits from their first four albums. Those are Rolie's distinctive pipes you hear on Santana's cover of Fleetwood Mac's 'Black Magic Woman'. Rolie's other role as the keyboardist meant that, during shows, he sang from behind his Hammond B3 organ cabinet. While Journey developed a core of dedicated fans, this setup didn't make for a dynamic live show. Herbie, the band, and most importantly, the record label were seeking hits, and having a charismatic lead vocalist was a necessary step in that direction.

Steve Perry Era

The band first turned to Robert Fleischman as its new vocalist. His story is covered in the recap of *Infinity*. Except for one song captured on the *Time*[3] box set, Fleischman doesn't appear on any Journey albums. In 1977, Herbie hired Steve Perry, a singer from northern California with a fantastic range and a distinctive voice, to replace Fleischman. Perry's considerable songwriting skills, as we will discuss throughout this volume, were as important as his voice. If we count the hiatus in the late 1980s and early 1990s, Perry was with the band for nearly 20 years. The Steve Perry era is usually divided into two distinct periods: the first with Gregg Rolie and the second with Jonathan Cain.

The Perry-Rolie period includes the albums *Infinity*, *Evolution*, *Departure*, *Dream, After Dream* and the live album *Captured*. This is the period where Journey experimented and crafted some of their best songs. They might not have been huge commercial successes, but for me, this is the sound of Journey that made me a fan.

Rolie, eager to begin a family and exit the grueling touring and recording pace that Herbie set for the band, exited after the *Departure* tour in 1980. Journey turned to the keyboardist from The Babys, Jonathan Cain, to replace him. Cain, a prolific wordsmith and composer, soon became the band's primary songwriter, partnering with both Perry and Schon on Journey's biggest commercial hits. The Perry-Cain period, the apex of their commercial success, includes *Escape, Frontiers, Raised On Radio* and *Trial By Fire*. Cain has been with the band since joining in 1981 and, as of 2024, he and Schon are the remaining members from the glory years of Steve Perry.

Steve Augeri Era

After *Trial By Fire*, Perry and Journey went their separate ways. Eager to keep the band alive, they hired Steve Augeri ('aw-jerry'), former lead singer of Tall Stories and Tyketto. His story is found in the *Arrival* recap. Augeri had the looks and could sing the big hits. From 1998 to the mid-2000s, the Augeri era includes *Arrival*, the EP *Red 13* and *Generations*. That last album features lead vocals from each member of Journey.

While on tour, Augeri's voice was failing, leading to a lip-synching controversy. The band hired Jeff Scott Soto to handle vocal duties for the remaining tour dates. This was a time of opportunity for the band, as Journey's popularity reignited with 'Don't Stop Believin'' appearing in movies, television shows and sporting events. By 2008, Journey needed to get back to recording and touring. However, Soto would not be their vocalist.

Arnel Pineda Era

The story of discovering Arnel Pineda is well-known to Journey fans, and it is covered in the recap of *Revelation*. The story involves false starts with other vocalists and the challenges of contacting Pineda, who was living in Manila. Once the singer was convinced to come to the United States, he spent a few days auditioning and became, and still is, the voice of Journey. He skillfully handles Perry's vocal nuances without doing a straight impersonation. Pineda's voice is expressive, and Journey have had some modest success with new music thanks to his vocal talents. The Pineda era includes *Revelation, Eclipse* and *Freedom*.

The Band Before 1975

San Francisco and the Bay Area of California were, in the late 1960s and early 1970s, the epicenter of a new musical language, fused from an array of musical traditions, including folk, rock, blues, psychedelic, jazz, country, Latin and soul. The roster of pioneering musical acts born of this swirling amalgam of influences and cultures is a poster child of musical diversity. Jefferson Airplane, Sly and the Family Stone, Big Brother and the Holding Company, Joan Baez, Grateful Dead, Moby Grape, Boz Scaggs, Steve Miller Band and Santana lead a long list of creative artists from the Bay Area.

In this world, Herbie Herbert started off as a musician but discovered he enjoyed the technical and business aspects of the industry. At 18, he became the road manager for Frumious Bandersnatch, a psychedelic band from the Bay Area, which, at different points, included future Journey members George Tickner (songwriter and guitarist) and Ross Valory (bassist).

Herbie met the powerful concert promoter and music business guru Bill Graham in the late 1960s. Whether or not Graham knew it, Herbie was enrolled at Graham's unofficial school of music business. From Graham, Herbie learned the ins and outs of booking venues, promoting shows, and understanding the fine print of contracts. Some of these lessons were learned from Graham's mistakes as well as his successes. Herbie, more than the band members themselves, is why Journey still exists. He made them into a money-making machine, letting them create while he handled the business side of things. Those written legal agreements kept Journey alive through much infighting and controversy over the coming 50 years.

Herbie worked on Santana's road crew, where he met Gregg Rolie and Neal Schon. Santana had fired their manager, Stan Marcum, in 1971 while on the *Santana III* tour. Drugs and different musical priorities led to the dissolution of Santana's original lineup. Rolie and Schon had played on *Caravanserai*, Santana's fourth album, but they left before the supporting 1972 tour began. Carlos Santana asked Herbie to manage the tour. However, without Rolie to sing the big hits, the tour became challenging to promote. Fans wanted 'Evil Ways' and 'Oye Como Va', not long, meandering instrumentals – ticket sales foundered as a result. Santana and Herbie agreed to part ways.

Herbie moved on to the Steve Miller Band, working as the road manager for their European tour. As Santana completed their disintegration, Herbie believed the teenage guitar prodigy Neal Schon – who shredded on *Santana (III)* and *Caravanserai* – would be an excellent focal point for constructing a band. After returning home from Europe, he considered how to create his dream musical act, a band that could be the Bay Area's answer to the Muscle Shoals Rhythm Section and Motown's Funk Brothers, and they would be named 'The Golden Gate Rhythm Section'. Herbie got to work.

For the 1973 New Year's Day *Sunshine Festival* in Oahu's Diamond Head Crater, Herbie had to fill the spot usually taken by Santana. He brought in Sly & The Family Stone drummer Greg Errico and future Jefferson Starship bassist

Pete Sears to play alongside Schon. Rolie also joined in before the set was completed. This was Herbie's dream on stage. Unfortunately, Errico and Sears had other commitments.

Herbie had to get to the serious work of assembling the band. One obvious target was Rolie, a founding member of Santana. In Herbie's plans, Rolie, a talented keyboardist who favored piano and his Hammond B3 organ, would be the lead singer. He had drifted back home to Seattle, attempting a restaurant business with his father, losing money and wishing he was on stage performing again. The veteran of Woodstock didn't need much coaxing from Herbie and Schon to bring him back to San Francisco.

Next, Herbie picked up the composer and guitarist George Tickner, formerly of Frumious Bandersnatch, a Bay Area band that released one album in the late 1960s, to play rhythm guitar. The bass player was someone Herbie knew well, Ross Valory, lately of The Steve Miller Band and with Frumious. For the drums, Herbie tapped Prairie Prince, who moved to the Bay Area from Arizona with his bandmates in The Tubes. He would only play on demo recordings and at a couple of gigs before returning to his friends in that band. In a moment of serendipity, veteran drummer Aynsley Dunbar, who had recently toured with David Bowie, was available and interested. He made the trip from England to the west coast. The five-member band was set.

After acknowledging that The Golden Gate Rhythm Section was perhaps not the best name, the band held a contest with a local radio station to find a new moniker. Nothing worked, so the story goes that roadie John Villanueva suggested 'Journey'. No one 'won' the contest, so the radio station faked a winner for the public.

Journey had their new name, a powerful lineup of veteran musicians and little early success. They toured constantly, opening for other acts and creating new music. They would not release their first record until 1975 and they wouldn't score a hit on the US charts until 1978, and that song, 'Wheel In The Sky', didn't even crack the top 40. Yet, by the middle of the 1980s, Journey would be one of the most popular and hardest-working bands in America, selling out stadiums and arenas and scoring hit after hit, until the personalities exploded and they went into a hiatus after the *Raised On Radio* tour.

Yet, the band didn't disintegrate because, by that time, Journey were owned by Nightmare Productions, and every member of Journey owned an equal share, including the manager, Herbie Herbert. To disband, they would need to make a legally binding business decision, which they avoided. A break was declared with no firm plans for a reunion. But before we get that far ahead, we should go back to the mid-1970s, when Herbie had not yet created Nightmare Productions and Journey were about to sign a record deal with Columbia.

Journey (1975)

Personnel:
Aynsley Dunbar: drums
Gregg Rolie: keyboards, lead vocals
Neal Schon: lead guitar, vocals
George Tickner: rhythm guitar
Ross Valory: bass, piano, vocals
Produced and engineered by Roy Halee for Spreadeagle Productions, a division of Herbert & Bramy, Inc.
Recorded by Mark Friedman and mastered by George Horn at CBS Studios, San Francisco
US release date: 1 April 1975
Highest chart position: US: 138
Running time: 36:37

Journey began recording their first album in November 1974. The noted producer, Roy Halee, received the keys to the San Francisco outpost of Columbia Records from its president, Clive Davis. Columbia looked to sign some of the rising talent from the Bay Area. Journey's musicianship, especially the youngster Neal Schon, impressed Halee and he signed them to a record deal.

Having someone of Halee's stature as the producer seemed like an incredible win for the young band. Halee had already won Grammys in 1970 for his work on Simon & Garfunkel's *Bridge Over Troubled Water*, including Album of the Year, Record of the Year and Best Engineering (non-Classical). He won for his production of 'Mrs. Robinson' from *Bookends* a year earlier. He recorded or produced a wide range of artists, from Peaches & Herb to the Yardbirds to Laura Nyro. Later, he engineered Simon's self-produced *Graceland* and *Rhythm Of The Saints*.

Given this track record, Halee seemed like a natural fit, but the album sounds muffled. *Journey* sound like Halee wanted these tracks to be spacey keyboard pieces that served as a backdrop for Schon's guitar. He succeeds at bringing out some fine work from the guitar prodigy, but the rest of the band, even the thundering drums of Aynsley Dunbar, sound subdued.

The main issue with this album is in the imbalance between the guitar-forward production and the muted presence of the other instruments. At times, it can sound like a Neal Schon solo effort. Halee admits to keeping Rolie and the Hammond B3 on the rhythm track, leaving Schon to shine alone. Cynthia Bowman, writing in a June 1975 issue of *Rolling Stone*, praised this decision because it 'prevents the lackluster vocals from intruding on the band's instrumental prowess.' Perhaps the vocals are 'lackluster' because of the mix. Rolie had a track record as the lead singer on Santana's early hit songs. He could have done the same on *Journey*.

However, the songs on *Journey* lack craft; there are no 'Evil Ways' here. Everyone seems to be happy to jam, showing their 'instrumental prowess'.

This improvisational approach, given that Schon doesn't read or write music, can sometimes be overlong, and Halee seems to recognize this. His method of solving the problem is to have these songs abruptly fade out or end. There are no ballads or rock hits here, though one song comes close to having commercial appeal. Ironically, what keeps the album from being eliminated from my rotation is the jamming. There are enjoyable moments during some of their long instrumental sections, but it's like listening to clips. Maybe if these moments were part of stronger songs, Journey would have found success much faster. They were young and still defining their sound. Neal Schon turned 21 a month before they released *Journey*. To be fair, Journey, at that time, did consider themselves a jam band. They had originally formed to work as a house band for a studio. Releasing hit singles wasn't their priority.

Released in April, it hit the *Billboard* Hot 200 in May 1975 and spent nine weeks on the charts before fading away.

The cover of *Journey* features the band in spacesuits, without helmets, photographed in various positions over an otherworldly mountain landscape. The reverse reveals the landscape is a tarp spread out on asphalt, and the band is shown kneeling over it. While clever, it doesn't have much to do with the album's contents. The most impressive things about these photos are Rolie's mutton chop sideburns and Schon's massive afro, which he will keep throughout the decade.

'Of A Lifetime' (Rolie, Schon, Tickner) 6:49

Opening with a repeated melody from Schon, the song, like many from these first albums, has memorable passages. I'm not a fan of vague and rambling lyrics like those found here. Every song does not have to make a profound philosophical statement, but the pretensions of such are hidden beneath metaphors that lack meaning, such as 'The mist is slowly lifting; the sound of life misplaced your mind'. This is a common complaint about the songs written before the coming of Steve Perry. Every track contains excellent guitar work, Rolie's distinctive vocals, the bed of sound laid down by the Hammond B3, and Dunbar crushing the drums. During the session for 'Of A Lifetime', Schon performed the solo, and when Halee recommended doubling it, Schon did the second version in one take. According to Schon, Halee was surprised that he could do it. This anecdote is often retold and made it to the liner notes on *Time*[3].

This song was a concert staple in that era and serves as a fine introduction to the band. This track is on *In The Beginning* and *Time*[3].

'In The Morning Day' (Rolie, Valory) 4:21

Valory, the bassist, opens this track playing the piano, which sounds like an early 1970s blues-tinged pop song. Rolie joins in with the organ and vocals, and the track marches along for three verses. Dunbar adds some rolls and Schon works in small guitar flourishes. Right before the two-minute mark, the band slip into jam mode. With a keyboard crescendo, they let it rip. The guitars pick up speed, Dunbar goes off on the drum kit and Valory adds a few bass runs while Rolie cranks up the Hammond B3, using it to build a sonic bed for the rest of the band. By the time Schon's solo kicks in, the song is rollicking towards an early fade out; these guys could have jammed for another five minutes.

While this is a classic cut for live performance, thanks to the high-energy turn midway through, with a little imagination, it could easily have been a single, but radio-friendly hits was not yet the goal. This is an example of what I find frustrating about Halee's production. Aside from having Dunbar's drums sound like toys on this track, he does a fade-out as Schon is heating up. Earlier, Rolie had ample time with the organ, and that's welcome, but maybe another minute or two of interplay between guitar and organ could have yielded some magic. Or Halee could have had them reintroduce the vocals, finishing strong with the repeated line, 'I want to give you happiness'. This feels like one of the album's missed opportunities.

'Kohoutek' (Schon, Rolie) 6:41
In the spring of 1973, a Czech astronomer, Luboš Kohoutek (pronounced 'ko-ho-tek'), discovered a new comet approaching the Sun. Given its proximity to Earth's orbit, experts expected it to be a dazzling astronomical event. As the world prepared to view Comet Kohoutek, Journey created an extended jam that they named in its honor. Unfortunately, the real Comet was a disappointment, not coming close to the predicted brightness, but Journey kept the name anyway, and the song became a staple at their concerts during this period.

The instrumental starts with a memorable keyboard arpeggio, repeatedly alternating between D and Gm, with Tickner and Valory providing the backdrop. Schon's guitar keeps things ethereal and spacey before the drums join in and the band circle the melody, rising higher. This is swiftly followed by an extended progressive rock workout after the two-minute mark. It's well executed, but it is overlong and stays rhythmically static. There is a sense of momentum lost when the work returns to the opening introspective melody for the final 90 seconds. The track ends with a synth-sounding coda after a brief rest to keep that ethereal feeling.

They released this track on a long-play (33 1/3) demo single with 'Topaz' on the B-side, intended for radio airplay at local powerhouse San Francisco radio station KSAN-FM. The track is on *In The Beginning* and *Time*[3].

'To Play Some Music' (Rolie, Schon) 3:15
What started off as a keyboard and guitar jam – originally called, in its earlier instrumental version, 'To Make Some Music' – became this poppy track. This is the closest the band came to a radio-friendly single on their debut. The chorus downshifts into an alternating minor chord, which adds interest and

keeps this from sounding cloyingly cheerful. It's a catchy pop tune that one wishes they had remade once they added a lead vocalist. I find the opening keyboard piece presages the hits of the arena rock bands of the late 1970s; think 'Blue Collar Man' from Styx. The song is about the sheer fun of playing before a crowd. Lyrically, it isn't very engaging. To paraphrase what Jonathan Cain would say years later, you must write songs about the audience, not about yourself. 'To Play Some Music' can sound like the audience is being instructed on how to listen, which makes for a rough sing-along experience. It doesn't cry out for engagement in the way that Bon Jovi's 'Raise Your Hands' does. Released with 'Topaz' on its B-side, the song did not chart, yet it remained popular at shows in the early years.

'Topaz' (Tickner) 6:10
George Tickner's only solo appearance as a songwriter is this instrumental. Tickner opens the song, slowly strumming out each chord one by one, accompanied by the bass. Schon joins shortly with some simple contemplative notes. Rolie adds some sustained chords from the B3 for depth, and for over a minute, all is calm. That's when 'Topaz' prepares for launch with a Dunbar drumroll. For a moment, the band appear to have settled into a jazzy, almost Latin vibe, but Schon and Dunbar thunder in for a few bars. The instrumental then alternates between slow keyboard and fast guitar phrases. At about the halfway point, the song shifts gears into a new section at a faster tempo and builds tension for another 90 seconds before returning to the opening slow melody. The drums rejoin, but the tempo stays slow, and Schon's soulful licks take the song to a fade out. For a six-minute instrumental, this is a satisfying listen. Schon's guitar wrings out the emotion of what could have been nothing more than an instrumental showcase. One of my favorites from this record. 'Topaz' is on *In The Beginning*.

'In My Lonely Feeling/Conversations' (Rolie, Valory) 4:54
The first part of this track, 'In My Lonely Feeling', is a short Rolie-penned bluesy tune where the lyrics question and then affirm that he is 'the master of my soul'. His excellent vocals and Dunbar's powerful drumming create an authentic emotional vibe. Around the 1:07 mark, Schon delivers the first of his two solos. It's 30 seconds of technically good but not very memorable playing. It serves as a contrast to the transition to Valory's 'Conversations'.

At the 2:13 mark, the second half of the track begins with a slow tempo and Schon doling out extended notes over Valory's melodic bass line, which shines throughout the track. A minute later, drums signal the increasing tempo and harder sound of an extended jam, adorned with a raging guitar solo, before slowing back down for the final 30 seconds. If you're not a Schon fan after listening to this, you will never be one. This track is on *In The Beginning*.

'Mystery Mountain' (Rolie, Tickner, Diane Valory) 4:22
Diane Valory, Ross's spouse, made her first songwriting credit appearance with 'Mystery Mountain'. She's more of a poet than a lyricist, which helps explain the song's volcano description as a 'mountain of mystery ... releasing the pressure built over the years. The mountain is crying hot lava tears. Molten rock created under vibrations of subterranean thunder'. Diane's poetry provides more explicit metaphors than 'Of A Lifetime' or 'In My Lonely Feeling' and it makes for a more memorable song.

After a rolling start that channels the Allman Brothers Band, with bass and rhythm guitar doubling each other during the intro and Schon and Dunbar building tension, Rolie sings of the mountain. The band sound lively and energetic. Valory's bass provides some melodic flair during the verses. Dunbar, around 2:00, while Rolie sings the final verse, plays some lightning-fast rolls on the snare, capturing the beginnings of an avalanche. It's a simple thing that brings the subject matter to life.

For the guitars, this is our last song with Tickner on rhythm, and on 'Mystery Mountain', he provides the bed of sound for the first half of the song. The true hero of this track is Schon. At the 2:20 mark, he takes over just as Rolie finishes singing. He builds up over the next 30 seconds and then unleashes his solo, which sounds like a homage to Duane Allman. It is terrific.

This leads us to the track's primary flaw. With Schon and company playing at a rolling boil, Halee slides them off the burner, fading the track out prematurely. What could Journey have done if they could have played this out? Maybe it would have rivaled some of the best jam tracks on the early Santana albums. This track is on *In The Beginning*.

Look Into The Future (1976)

Personnel:
Aynsley Dunbar: drums, percussion
Gregg Rolie: keyboards, lead vocals
Neal Schon: guitars, background vocals
Ross Valory: bass, vocals
Produced by Journey for Spreadeagle Productions, a division of Herbert & Bramy, Inc.
Associate producer and engineer: Glen Kolotkin
Recorded by Mark Friedman and mastered by George Horn at CBS Studio, San Francisco
US release date: January 1976
Highest chart position: US: 100
Running time: 41:41

The pattern that manager Herbie Herbert set for the band would repeat until the end of the *Frontiers* tour. Journey would perform on the road for nine months and then create an album for three months. It was a hard pace and would take its toll on each band member. The first casualty of this approach was rhythm guitarist George Tickner. He left the band in 1975 and went to Stanford to become a surgical technician. Rather than hire a new guitarist, Journey became a quartet. Band members began taking voice lessons and vowed to tighten up their songwriting for their sophomore effort. They went back to CBS Studios in late 1975 to make *Look Into The Future,* this time self-producing.

A conscious decision to include shorter, radio-friendly songs led to half the tracks being around four minutes or less, crammed onto the album's first side. Columbia wanted hits, but they had difficulty generating ad copy for the record. Telling radio stations and reviewers that Journey's sound was 'heavy space' (lifted from a *Billboard* review) didn't inspire much airplay.

The few critics who reviewed the album stated that it was an improvement over the debut, but their enthusiasm stopped there. One reviewer was concerned that the shorter songs on the album's first half would not hold up in concert, predicting that 'they will fall into prolonged guitar solos and deteriorate into crashing racket.' If you have seen them live or watched videos from those mid-1970s shows, you'd believe that the California-based critic had seen them live, too.

The cover features blue-tinted full-body photos of the individual band members wearing matching jumpsuits. They are in a beige room with infinite rooms stretching back through doorways behind the figures, and there's a crystal ball in the foreground reflecting all of this. The cover's reverse is identical except that the bodies are silhouettes. Louis Bramy, Herbert's partner in Spreadeagle Productions, created the concept to match the album title. The sleeve replicates the back cover, and the reverse is a set of four band photos taken on the same set used for the cover images.

'On A Saturday Nite' (Rolie) 3:57
Rolie's piano opens this tune, which signals their commitment to recording songs to fit the four-minute window that AM and hit radio stations preferred. This is the first traditionally constructed single by Journey, with a bridge featuring a toned-down Schon solo. Rolie's voice comes through more clearly here than on the debut album. The track lacks personality and emotion. The chorus should be a rousing concert sing-along, but they don't quite build up the song's partying nature. Instead, we get the trite 'on a Saturday night, everything is alright'. What might have been a modest chart hit ends up sounding like album filler. This was released as a single (stereo b/w mono versions) and did not chart. The track is on *In The Beginning*.

'It's All Too Much' (George Harrison) 4:03
The Beatles put this hazy, spacey Harrison chant on *Yellow Submarine*. Journey transform it into a rocking pop song. Rolie's more assertive vocal delivery is noticeable; his chants of 'hey, hey, hey' and 'no, no, no' on the bridge sound energetic and convincing. It gallops along as Schon and Rolie create a 'wall of sound' with the guitar and organ. That opening guitar melody is pure pop-rock. Schon repeats the melody around the 3:00 mark.

Journey's only cover on a studio album is a clever remake, bearing little resemblance to the more deliberately psychedelic original. I find it an enjoyable pop tune. It was released as a B-side to 'She Makes Me (Feel Alright)' and collected on *In The Beginning*.

'Anyway' (Rolie) 4:10
Another Rolie composition opens with his keyboard and Valory's bass slowly setting the stage for Schon's extended Moody Blues-like passages. It's an effective approach, creating a haunting sound, even with Dunbar's drumming at times threatening the laid-back mood. This song is the closest they come to realizing the vision of 'heavy space'. Rolie's lyrics don't delve much deeper than the generic song title, which is endlessly repeated in the chorus. This track is on *In The Beginning*.

'She Makes Me (Feel Alright)' (music: Schon; words: Rolie, Alex Cash) 3:10
Schon launches a rocker that sounds like Bad Company or Humble Pie. His guitar takes center stage. Even Dunbar's drums take a rare backseat. The lyrics, from Rolie and the San Francisco singer/guitarist/songwriter Alex Cash (sometimes spelled 'Kash', short for 'Kashevaroff'), are about a woman's looks and whether the guy can convince her to spend a little time with him. This is not a common Journey subject in these early days. Many of their songs have an imprecise philosophical take or the generic party vibe of 'To Play Some Music' or 'On A Saturday Nite', so hearing them drift into topics like love and desire is something new. The song rips along its three-

minute run time before a fadeout that, for once, sounds natural and planned. This was released as a single with B-side 'It's All Too Much' but did not chart.

'You're On Your Own' (music: Schon, Tickner/words: Rolie) 5:52
The boys do a decent impersonation of The Beatles here, with Rolie sounding like John Lennon in the early verses. Schon's guitar tone is akin to the guitars in 'I Want You (She's So Heavy)'. George Tickner's compositional work appears on the first three studio albums, although he only played on *Journey*. Time signature changes, such as the move between 4/4 and 6/8 on this track, appear in nearly all the tracks he had a hand in writing. These changes create energy for the instrumental breaks, usually from Schon, but here, as Schon finishes a short guitar solo at the 3:14 mark, Rolie's B3 takes center stage for the next half minute.

When Rolie affects a stylistic vocal with 'We'll try to make up your mind' over and over during the fade, the song could be mistaken for an outtake from *Abbey Road*. I think it is one of the more interesting tracks on the early records, showcasing the band's instrumental skill and Rolie's evolving vocals. This track is on *In The Beginning*.

'Look Into The Future' (music: Schon; words: Rolie, Diane Valory) 8:10
This is one of the band's longest tracks, and it deserves much more love and attention. Schon was 21 when he created this. The sound of early Journey is sometimes reminiscent of Cream, but here, it evokes Lynyrd Skynyrd, specifically the first half of 'Free Bird'. Schon keeps the guitar subdued – Schon's solos are examples of control and sincerity – and Valory and Dunbar are also understated in their playing, limiting the flourishes.

Rolie and Diane Valory wrote the lyrics, which explore a person's difficulty in trying to navigate life – but these things seem to work themselves out. The final repeated line of 'It's right around the corner, just around the corner' is poignant and works powerfully with the music, which ends naturally rather than fading out. This is one of my all-time favorite Journey songs. The track is on *In The Beginning*. If you'd like to hear an excellent remake, check out Gregg Rolie's 2019 solo album *Sonic Ranch*.

'Midnight Dreamer' (music: Schon; words: Rolie) 5:13
Here's a barn-burning rocker from Schon and Rolie that sounds straight out of the 1960s, like some up-tempo Steppenwolf or Grand Funk. Continuing the lyrical content of 'She Makes Me (Feel Alright)', this five-minute track is done with the vocals by the 1:30 mark. 'Midnight Dreamer' provides a platform for some extended solos and jamming. Schon strums over the groove laid down by Valory and Dunbar, and Rolie kicks off the solos on piano. The keyboard transitions to synthesizer while Schon steadily increases the guitar volume, building anticipation for his solo.

Around the 3:15 mark, the synthesizer gives way to the lead guitar. Schon plays with his usual ferocity, but this solo leaves me cold. He repeats licks three or four times at various points, and I find it musically uninteresting. It slows the momentum and doesn't increase the musical tension. I find myself wondering when the track will end every time I hear it. The song concludes with a stray smack on the floor tom as the mic cuts off.

'I'm Gonna Leave You' (music: Schon, Rolie, Tickner; words: Rolie) 6:58
The final track is another Tickner co-write, this time with Schon and Rolie. The opening sounds like we're going to hear a cover of REO Speedwagon's 'Ridin' The Storm Out' but instead shifts into something even more familiar. While Rolie is working the keyboards, the bass and drums play a familiar 5/4 rhythm. In between bass notes, the drums roll while Schon follows with a scorching guitar. They repeat this pattern for the first half minute of the song, and fans will recognize the similarity to the opening of Kansas's 'Carry On Wayward Son'; Journey released *Look Into The Future* ten months before *Leftoverture*. Kansas had been doing a few shows with Journey, and while no one has accused anyone of musical plagiarism, the similarities are undeniable.

However, the similarities end with this riff. Kansas's song is polished and radio-friendly enough to become a hit. 'I'm Gonna Leave You' is a mostly forgotten track whose primary claim to fame is sounding like the song that came later. Yet, it has some merit. Valory lays down a strong foundation in one of his better early performances. The chorus is satisfying, with Dunbar and Schon doing their usual pyrotechnics. During the bridge, Rolie shows his prowess on the organ. By the 3:45 mark, the opening section returns, and the original melody resumes. The final two minutes are another workout for Schon. There is nothing wrong with the fretwork, but after two or three solos, it can fatigue the ear. There is no doubting the band's musicianship, but they're quickly approaching a 'find a hit or you're done' message from their record label. This track is on *In The Beginning* and *Time*[3].

Next (1977)

Personnel:
Aynsley Dunbar: drums, percussion
Gregg Rolie: keyboards, lead vocals
Neal Schon: electric and acoustic guitars, lead vocals
Ross Valory: bass, background vocals
Produced by Journey for Nightmare Productions, Inc.
Recorded and mixed at His Master's Wheels, San Francisco
Recording and mixing engineer: Smiggy
Mastered by Bruce Botnick at Capitol Recording Studios, Hollywood
US release date: 28 February 1977
Highest chart position: US: 85
Running time: 37:33

Between *Look Into The Future* and *Next*, Herbie Herbert and Lou Bramy parted ways. Spreadeagle Productions, which had managed Journey and other acts, was no more. This act was a key step on Journey's road to financial success as Herbie became the sole band manager. Lou Bramy took the firm's other band, Yesterday & Tomorrow, who would become familiar to audiences as Y&T and score a minor MTV hit in the 1980s with 'Summertime Girls'. Bramy kept the Spreadeagle name.

Herbie created Nightmare Productions, Inc. back in 1973 before it became the ownership entity of Journey, with five equal partners: the four band members and Herbert. As the executive, Herbie ran the business side of things, though he didn't ignore the music. They needed to sell records and tickets. None of the first three albums topped 250,000 units sold. Each album charted higher than the last but *Next* spent less time on the *Billboard* Hot 200 than *Look Into The Future*, lasting only ten weeks in the spring of 1977. Journey would again self-produce the album, but this time, they recorded at His Master's Wheels.

Engineer Smiggy (Robert Smith) stepped in to replace Glen Kolotkin. Smiggy, a German-born British session guitarist who would work with Jerry Garcia and did live engineering for Robin Trower, assisted Journey in taking advantage of Elliot Mazer's newly acquired equipment and studio, His Master's Wheels, in San Francisco. The studio had originally been a plastics factory, so it had a garage door and delivery dock. Mazer had a truck-based mobile studio he kept there, thus the oddly named studio. Mazer had also acquired a new console, tape machines and other equipment for the studio, which Smiggy and the band used for this album and *Infinity*.

The band had been touring relentlessly, nine months each year, and while they built a small following, it wasn't enough for Columbia. Herbie gave a brutally honest three-point critique of the band to Ben Fong-Torres: one, they were subpar songwriters; two, they were not dynamic on the stage; and three, they could not sing. Rolie's voice was suffering from the constant touring.

Before recording *Look Into The Future*, Herbie sent the guys to Bianca Thornton for vocal lessons. The vocals do sound better on the second album, but they lack power and flair. Lady Bianca helped them get in touch with their emotions and carry a tune. For *Next*, Neal Schon takes lead vocals on a couple of tracks. It helped vary their sound, but it didn't help them find additional record buyers.

Admittedly, the band members weren't feeling the same urgency as Herbie. In a 1980 interview with *Rolling Stone*, Schon told Fong-Torres: 'Jamming was the easiest thing we could do.' Rolie said, 'Some of it was blowing our chops and playing for ourselves.' They were happy to be jamming for appreciative audiences. Yet, they all knew that to keep making records for Columbia, they would have to do something with their sound. They'd have to address all three of Herbie's criticisms.

The art for *Next* is simple, featuring a band portrait on the front on a gray field. The reverse is another photo of the band kneeling and laughing in an outdoor setting that looks like a California valley. Bruce Steinberg provided art direction and photography and worked on the design with Ellie Oberzil. What's interesting here is the sleeve art for the vinyl record, credited to Mansfield, depicting a black-and-white bordered triangle with a sky-blue fill. Bird wings come out of each side of the triangle, while the base sports tail feathers. Is this part of Herbie's vision for a series of wing-themed covers? This image is not included in the CD's booklet or cover.

'Spaceman' (music: Rolie; words: Dunbar, Rolie) 3:59
The only single released from *Next* begins with the bass and a simple piano melody. Schon adds guitar accents, and the song sounds like Journey performing an Elton John tune (which other critics have noted). Instead of Taupin's lyrics, we have Dunbar's first songwriting contribution, joining Rolie to write the lyrics. The track is subtitled 'A song for hang-gliders'. Rolie singing 'I'm not a spaceman' is an oddly negative way of describing hang-gliding, exemplified further by 'I'm a cosmopolitan right-handed wingless man'. According to David Hamilton Golland, the lyrics are a response to a critic describing their music on the prior two albums as 'heavy space'. The music and the vocals sound like a reach for AM radio airplay, perhaps a subconscious homage to *Honky Chateau*'s 'Rocket Man'. This was their best chance on *Next* to break into the *Billboard* Top 100 singles chart, and it didn't make it. 'Spaceman' was released as a single with B-side 'Nickel And Dime' and included on *In The Beginning*.

'People' (music: Schon and Rolie; words: Dunbar) 5:19
After a simple two-chord opening, 'People' gives the illusion of being a typical Journey extended instrumental, spending over a minute in a leisurely repeated, easy-on-the-ear F-G-C sequence used in many pop songs. At the 2:57 mark, after Rolie's vocals have run their course, Schon delivers what he

calls 'the easiest thing in the world' in a well-played solo that goes on for nearly a minute. Lyrically, 'People' is a short, cynical complaint about how we all fall short of our potential. However, Rolie sings it with a hint of wry humor. The extended guitar solo makes us forget that negativity. The song returns to the opening melody before a fade and then an abrupt tutti to close it out. The track is on *In The Beginning*.

'I Would Find You' (music: Schon; words: Schon, Tena Austin) 5:52
Opening with a keyboard sequence that immediately suggests the beginning of Peter Gabriel's 'Sledgehammer', 'I Would Find You' quickly parts ways with that monster hit. Gabriel's song goes quiet before the keyboard and brass flourish truly begin the tune. Here, after the opening keys, Journey take this to even quieter contemplative levels, setting us up for Schon's first turn as lead vocalist.

Cowritten by Schon and his then-wife Tena Austin, this is about two people physically separated but spiritually connected. After about three and a half minutes of Schon's quiet, growly vocals, he lights up the guitar with an effective solo that is indicative of his best work to come during the Steve Perry days.

Things downshift at the final minute, and the song fades. I admit that I was disappointed that the track faded out. It seemed like Schon had plenty of gas left in the tank. Were they so concerned with avoiding jamming that they didn't want anything to exceed six minutes? This is one that I would have liked to have heard live.

'Here We Are' (Rolie) 4:16
A wash of keyboards has you wondering for a moment if Steve Perry is about to belt out some early version of 'Oh Sherrie'. As the synthesizers fade, Rolie quietly plays the song's actual melody, Dunbar works the cymbals and a song that would not sound out of place on a Beatles album from the mid-1960s begins. 'Here We Are' is a harbinger of things to come, especially after Jonathan Cain joins the band, with its positive message of keeping your head up and persevering. The band even harmonize at a couple of points. While the tune plods a little, it keeps its optimistic sentiment – but this seems a tame way to end the album's first side.

'Hustler' (music: Rolie; words: Dunbar) 3:15
Schon's six-second intro solo sets the tone, and the song only lets up during the verses as Rolie sings in the gaps between the halting, crunchy chords. Rolie's voice isn't quite up for a song that would sound better with either a tenor scream or a bass growl. The lyrics penned by Aynsley Dunbar are straight out of the adolescent fantasies of a would-be lothario. According to touring legend, Dunbar enjoyed using his rockstar status with groupies, but with lines like 'screamin' women love me, just can't resist' and 'so lock up

your women, like you know you should', we are not in Journey's usual lyric territory. Schon's solos show off his lightning-fast fretwork and dominate the second half of this short track, with Dunbar keeping pace. It's an interesting comparison with songs like Van Halen's 'I'm The One' or Mountain's 'Never In My Life'.

'Next' (music: Schon, Rolie; words: Dunbar, Rolie, Heidi Cogdell) 5:27
The title track, for me, is where we start hearing a more mature, commercial version of Journey. The 30-second introduction builds upon a driving beat with guitar chords; so far, this could easily be mistaken for a lead track on *Escape* or *Frontiers*. The song downshifts into a repeated riff, still melodic but not as propulsive, for the next 30 seconds. Around the one-minute mark, we slow down one more time as Rolie sings the first verse accompanied by his piano.

The substantial difference between this track and all the others on these first three albums is the lyrics. We go from the un-Journey sentiment in 'Hustler' to this song of romantic loss and separation. It heralds their compositional approach to the early Perry-era albums.

'Nickel And Dime' (Tickner, Valory, Schon, Rolie) 4:12
This Tickner-cowritten instrumental is another leftover from the *Journey* days (just as 'I'm Gonna Leave You' and 'You're On Your Own' are debut album leftovers included on *Look Into The Future*). Each song Tickner cowrote has a little more musical complexity than the usual early Journey track.

After opening with a 20-second waltz (reminding me of Richard Rodgers' 'My Favorite Things'), the band launch into the 5/4 section of the instrumental. Neal Schon sounds like Joe Satriani for a half minute, albeit nine years before Satch's debut, *Not Of This Earth*. Check out Satriani tracks like 'Circles' from *Surfing With The Alien* or the title cut from *Crystal Planet* to hear a similar style.

Right after the song's one-minute mark, the time signature jumps again, and Journey sound like *Moving Pictures*-era Rush. Schon's guitar tone sounds uncannily like Rush's Alex Lifeson. As they continued to mature, it's interesting to contemplate what Journey could have done before their decisive turn to rhythm & blues-influenced pop rock on the next album.

According to the liner notes of *Time*[3], 'Nickel And Dime' had a third section in 7/4 that the band omitted, thus giving the track this title for the five- and ten-time signatures. 'Nickel And Dime' is a classic Journey cut and is on *In The Beginning* and *Time*[3].

'Karma' (music: Schon, Rolie; words: Dunbar) 5:06
'Karma' is about the universal theme of a man begging a girl to do what future Journey singer Steve Perry will refer to as 'the lovin' things'. The track begins with the slightest hint of Foreigner's 'Jukebox Hero' when Schon's

guitar ripsaws its way through the intro as the band settle into a minor-key blues groove. Schon has primary vocal duties, too, and he belts out 'Oh, baby' with plenty of swagger, but this serves as a reminder that they need a lead singer. At the end of the track, the music fades, returns, and fades again. They have fine musical ideas, and though they sound brilliant at times, these songs are not well-crafted at this point. While 'Karma' is worth a listen, it isn't all that memorable.

Related Track
'Cookie Duster' (Valory) 4:19
This Ross Valory bass-driven instrumental jam, recorded for *Next*, was cut for space and stylistic fit. Valory plays a walking bass line throughout the track as a bed for Rolie's B3 and piano. It's like a jazzy version of a Booker T. and The M.G.s' instrumental. Schon's contributions are understated until just before the two-minute mark when he crashes in with some flashy playing. Dunbar's drumming stands out here, too, showing a feel for this music. After his Journey days came to an end, he continued to be a sought-after drummer. It's a shame this didn't track didn't make the cut, but it has a jazz fusion feel that doesn't fit in with the rest of the record. Luckily, it is on *Time*[3].

Infinity (1978)

Personnel:
Aynsley Dunbar: drums, percussion
Steve Perry: lead vocals
Gregg Rolie: keyboards, vocals
Neal Schon: guitar, vocals
Ross Valory: bass, vocals
Produced and mixed by Roy Thomas Baker for RTB (Audio/Visual) Productions, Ltd. at His Master's Wheels, San Francisco, and Cherokee Studios, Los Angeles.
Engineer: Geoffrey Workman
First album with Kelley & Mouse artwork
US release date: 20 January 1978
Highest chart position: US: 21; Certified 3x Platinum
Running time: 36:28

After the limited success of *Next* in 1977, the patience of the executives at Columbia Records had worn thin. Journey's albums each sold around 200,000 copies, not that the band were an overall unsuccessful act. They were a popular opener and had a dedicated fan base. They toured constantly, pairing up with the likes of Emerson, Lake & Palmer, Foreigner and Electric Light Orchestra and, ironically, doing a tour of Europe with Santana. Herbie knew the band needed a charismatic lead singer, someone to work the crowd, sing the songs, and hopefully help them write some radio-friendly hits to drive record sales. If they didn't, being dropped by Columbia was a certainty.

In June 1977, Herbie brought in southern California-based singer Robert Fleischman, who rehearsed with the band and joined their current tour supporting *Next*. Fleischman's time on tour was challenging. The band would open their sets, as usual, without a separate lead singer. After three or four songs, Fleischman would make his entrance. Hardcore Journey fans, were hostile to the new lead singer. Fleischman persisted, and for a few months, it appeared that Journey had their man.

Things get murky at this point in the story. Revisionist versions of what happened next are many, from Fleischman being too demanding to a struggle between management. Herbie didn't manage Fleischman; that job belonged to the successful promoter, Barry Fey. Knowing what we know of Herbie's plans for Journey, we can safely say Herbert found this untenable for Nightmare Productions.

Another side of the story is how Herbie came to learn of Steve Perry, lately the lead singer of the Los Angeles-based band Alien Project. When that band was on the verge of signing a record deal, the bass player died in an automobile accident. Perry was ready to give up his musical dreams, but his mother convinced him to stick with it, so he kept at it, sending demos and looking for work.

Did Herbie already know of Perry? According to Herbie, Perry was always in the back of his mind since he heard him on demos, but once Perry became available, Herbie had to figure out how to remove Fleischman. Another story is that Michael Dilbeck at Columbia Records gave Herbie a Perry demo and told him that, for the sake of Journey continuing with the label, he should bring Perry in as his lead singer.

Herbie's nature would not permit him to admit that someone else provided direction on what Journey should do for a lead singer. Whether Dilbeck or Herbie or both heard the demo, it would be folly to ignore the talent. Ultimately, it doesn't matter because Herbie knew this voice was a game-changer.

Herbie clandestinely brought Perry in as a 'Portuguese cousin' of road crew member Jack Villanueva. While Fleischman was away from the band, Perry stood in during sound checks. Herbie told the band that he would be their new lead singer. Herbie fired Fleischman for the minor infraction of asking for more attention during the live performances. He was gone by October. Steve Perry sang onstage as a member of the band on 28 October 1977.

There is another story in which office manager John Villanueva (Jack's brother) warned Herbert that bringing on Perry would tear the band apart. It would take about a decade and tens of millions of dollars later for that to happen, but for now, Journey had entered a new phase of their creative and recording careers.

The band went back to His Master's Wheels to record, but instead of self-producing, Dilbeck introduced them to CBS's newly hired gun, Roy Thomas Baker (RTB), the English producer of acts such as Nazareth, Hawkwind, and, most famously, Queen, where he piloted five of their albums, including *A Night At The Opera*, which contains the iconic 'Bohemian Rhapsody'. The band had been writing music with Fleischman, including what would be their first hit, 'Wheel In The Sky'. Perry, a talented songwriter on his own, brought in some of his work to try out, including 'Lights'. His first co-write with Neal Schon, 'Patiently', showed how well these two would collaborate. The band were ready to record.

While RTB receives the producing credit, the band would single out engineer Geoff Workman for his skill at getting the sound they were after. RTB was the master of the multi-track approach to instrumental and vocal work, but Workman, true to his name, did the heavy lifting. Thanks to an alcohol-driven fire extinguisher duel between stage manager Scott Ross and RTB, they ruined the studio's mixing board, forcing them to move to Cherokee Studios in Los Angeles to finish the album. For many fans, myself included, *Infinity* was our introduction to Journey. Their musicianship was as fine as ever, and Perry brought his unique vocals and excellent songwriting, transforming Journey into a fundamentally different band.

Infinity represented step one in Herbie's master plan. He had sketched a sequence of seven albums, beginning with *Infinity*, that included a relentless touring and recording schedule. Under Herbie's guiding hand, Journey would become a ubiquitous brand. That began with the album cover designs. Contracting Alton Kelley and Stanley Mouse, famous Bay Area artists known for their iconic posters and album covers – most notably for The Grateful Dead – they enhanced the wing motif from the Mansfield sketch on *Next* to create the definitive image that dominates Journey iconography to the present day. Herbie wanted the record-buying public to see the wings and know they were looking at a Journey product.

Beginning their tour on the album's release date in Chicago, the band toured until 2 September 1978, ending in San Francisco. Herbie made the crucial decision that Journey would be the headliner, not the opening act, on this tour. Hard-rocking bands such as Montrose and Van Halen opened for them. *Infinity* sold half a million albums by May 1978 and would top a million by October, ultimately going triple platinum. Herbie's plan was succeeding beyond their highest hopes.

'Lights' (Perry, Schon) 3:10
Perry brought this song about Los Angeles with him. They reworked the lyrics to make it about San Francisco, and it has become the city's de facto anthem, regularly played at San Francisco Giants baseball games. Opening with a simple melody from Schon, Perry introduces himself to Journey listeners by singing the chorus. The tune reveals Perry's habit of emphasizing vowels in interesting musical ways, with 'city' becoming 'sit-tay' and 'bay' receiving a few extra syllables ('bay-ee-yay-ay'). The Baker-trademarked overdubbed backing vocals signal that this is a new Journey – a radio-friendly Journey. They slow things down, limit Dunbar's drumming to the needs of the song, ask no more of Valory than underscoring the beat and keep the instrumental indulgences from running wild. Schon's strong emotional solo is an album highlight.

'Lights', released as the third single (with B-side 'Somethin' To Hide') from *Infinity*, peaked at number 68 on the *Billboard* Hot 100 chart, where it stayed for a respectable 17 weeks. It is on the *Greatest Hits*.

'Feeling That Way' (Perry, Rolie, Dunbar) 3:27
A discarded tune from the *Next* sessions with new lyrics and RTB's stacked vocals for the chorus, this song excellently uses both Rolie's and Perry's voices. (Like many Journey fans, I count this as among my personal favorites). Rolie opens on piano and sings alone, which is a respectful callback back to the first three albums. Here, Rolie's voice is not relegated to the background but embraced for its strengths. We are over 30 seconds in when Dunbar leads the entire band in and Perry belts out the chorus: 'When the summer's gone, she'll be there, standing by the light' – which comes out 'lie-yite'. Perry and Rolie harmonize throughout. Schon's solo during the bridge is tight and understated, yet technically flawless. Dunbar and Valory up the ante as the song builds to its conclusion – with Perry's 'whoa, whoa, whoa' and 'ma, ma,

ma' wails over repeats of backing vocals singing the song title – where there is a dramatic pause, and everyone sings 'feeling that way' one final time with an audio smash cut to...

'Anytime' (Rolie, Roger Silver, Fleischman, Schon, Valory) 3:28
...'Ooh, anytime that you want me ... Ooh, anytime that you need me'. Thus, the a cappella beginning of the song seems forever tied to 'Feeling That Way', whether in concert or on the radio. The 'wall of sound' track rolls on, with Rolie doing most of the vocal work. On video and in concert, Rolie would stand on his bench with outstretched arms above the organ cabinet as he sang, 'I'm standing here, with my arms a mile wide'. Perry has a vocal part that powerfully introduces the bridge, where Schon once again executes an excellent, understated solo. These new compositions are limiting Schon's solos with clear boundaries while using him to supply color and texture. The song fades with the guitar repeating the primary chord progression (E-D-A). The fadeout feels natural instead of an attempt to prevent the band from doing extended jams.

Robert Fleischman has a writing credit, and bootleg recordings can be found of him singing the lead vocal part. Without the studio production treatment, it sounds thin and raw. Roger Silver, a Bay Area writer, contributed some lyrics.

'Anytime' was the second single released from this album (with the B-side 'Can Do') and peaked at 83 on the *Billboard* charts, lasting only four weeks. Along with 'Feeling That Way', it is collected on *Time^3* and *Greatest Hits 2*.

'La Do Da' (Perry, Schon) 3:01
Even on a 36-minute album, you can't keep Schon from having at least one track where he unleashes his guitar. 'La Do Da' is spelled with diacritic marks on the record to let us know it is pronounced 'lah-doo-day'. Schon stated during a radio interview that this song was for Ted Nugent fans; his high-note lead guitar and the non-stop driving shuffle sound a bit like the Motor City Madman, only with some sterling lead vocals from Perry. There's no depth here, only straight hard rock with a touch of 1960s Motown coming through in both the lyrics ('Something about you, baby...') and Perry's delivery.

'Patiently' (Perry, Schon) 3:20
Famous for being the first song written by Perry and Schon, according to Perry, it only took an hour to craft in a hotel room in Denver. It opens with an elegant guitar and vocals with lyrics that sound as if they were stolen from a Jonathan Cain notebook. This initially sounds like a ballad, but after 90 seconds of a sappy love song that includes some fine piano from Rolie, Schon steps on the drive pedal and is joined by the rhythm section. For a minute, the track heats up, with Perry belting out 'One in a million' and Schon delivering another restrained solo. Then, the song cools back into the

opening guitar and piano melody, and Perry closes it out to end side one. This is collected on *Time³* and *Greatest Hits 2*.

'Wheel In The Sky' (Schon, Fleischman, Diane Valory) 4:11
Robert Fleischman's most significant contribution to the band is this song, originally based on Diane Valory's poem 'Wheels In My Mind' about missing Ross out on the road. Fleischman reworked it to be about the grind of touring. Lyrically, it is one of Journey's most mature non-love songs. Written in a minor key, Schon plays a tasteful melody before the band join. Perry's vocals reflect the weariness and angst of extended time on the road. The stacked vocals on the choruses and another classy bridge from Schon helped Journey have their first radio hit. The album's lead single (US B-side 'Can Do', non-US B-side 'Patiently'), the song peaked at 57 on the *Billboard* charts in the spring of 1978 and lasted for eight weeks. This classic is collected on *Time³* and *Greatest Hits*.

'Somethin' To Hide' (Perry, Schon) 3:26
The second of three minor key tunes that start side two of *Infinity*, this odd number from Perry and Schon was rarely performed live. It plods along, and Perry must hit some remarkably high notes in the chorus – this would have been a struggle to perform at scores of shows per year. Rolie delivers some fine piano playing, and after the end of the guitar solo, around the 1:42 mark, the group's vocals are reminiscent of 10cc's opening vocals in 'The Things We Do For Love'. Perry works his way through some chorus repeats and vocalizes over Schon's final flourishes. It's a challenging song and not among their best, though Perry has said that he loved it.

'Winds Of March' (Matthew Schon, Schon, Fleischman, Rolie, Perry) 5:03
You would be forgiven if you thought this song was called 'You Are My Child'. Instead, the title comes from the line, 'You came in like the winds of March', which is only heard twice during this complex tune. It started life as a Schon, Rolie and Fleischman song, with Matthew Schon, Neal's father, supplying the chord progressions. Written in C minor to reflect the song's mood, it has a haunting acoustic guitar and piano intro. The track begins as another ballad, albeit with terrific music, when, at the 2:55 mark, Journey revert to their jamming ways of the first three albums. Schon cranks up the volume and Rolie lets fly with the Hammond B3 – for a minute, it feels like we are back on a *Journey* track. It's a glorious moment for the band and makes 'Winds Of March' a true bridge between old and new Journey. The song closes as it opens with Schon on acoustic and Rolie on piano. It's a terrific tune that is sadly omitted from any of their major collections.

'Can Do' (Perry, Valory) 2:38
Perry admitted that he does not remember too much about this song other than the title, which means that Ross Valory likely did the lion's share of the

writing. It's a hard rock song with a driving beat; the verses, while shallow and typical, outshine the silly chorus. As a young listener, I could not get into singing the Rolie-dominated chorus – 'You can do what you want to, you can do if you try' – with the rising sustained notes at the end of each line. Nothing in this song highlights Perry's singing. While rarely performed live, it does feature, like every track on this album, a skillful, if not thrilling, solo from Schon.

'Opened The Door' (Perry, Rolie, Schon) 4:36
The most notable aspect of *Infinity* in comparison to the first three albums is the decreased tempo. 'Lights' and 'Somethin' To Hide' barely move compared to the sprawling instrumentals from the pre-Perry days. 'Opened The Door' continues this slow walk by opening with the cymbal and a simple piano melody, which is doubled on guitar. Perry sings the soulful words – 'girl, you came to me, touched my life' – holding 'girl' for a whole note or two. The song continues like this until we get to the chorus. The stacked vocals don't add much interest. Neither does Schon's guitar work nor Dunbar's flange effect on his drums. The song fades out and the album is complete, ending not quite as impressively as it began.

Related Tracks
'For You' (Rolie, Schon, Fleischman) 3:57
The only Journey song sung by Robert Fleischman on an official release is this solid pop-rock tune. Would Journey have been successful with Fleischman? While it's speculation, there is a good chance they would have found success. The evidence is found on *Infinity*. Fleischman's contributions to 'Wheel In The Sky', 'Anytime' and 'Winds Of March' led to tracks with more pop-rock orientation than their earlier work. Fleischman has a good voice, but it's not as distinctive as Steve Perry's.

Fleischman's singing has been compared to that of Robert Plant, but on this track, he reminds me of Jefferson Starship lead singer Mickey Thomas. (Thomas joined Jefferson Starship in 1979, shortly after they got a new drummer named Aynsley Dunbar.) Fleischman hits the high notes without effort. The chorus, featuring Rolie's signature tones, would have worked well with RTB's multitracking technique. It's an enjoyable sing-along and might have been a modest hit.

When Fleischman left the band, he kept the song and included it on his 1979 solo album *Perfect Stranger*, though he retitled it 'All For You' and featured Neal Schon on guitar. The Journey demo version is collected on *Time^3*.

'Velvet Curtain' or 'Let Me Stay' (Rolie, Dunbar) 1:03
Included on *Time^3*, this little demo outtake is the first minute of the 'Feeling That Way' entry on the box set. The idea here was to show how Journey

reworked their songs until they were ready for the album. Journey had an instrumental called 'Velvet Curtain', which Rolie turned into 'Let Me Stay' – a variation of 'Feeling That Way' with a different chorus: 'Please let me stay, just another day, please let me stay'. Perry worked with the song and the lyrics that became 'When the summer's gone, she'll be there, standing by the light'. It's a curious excerpt. Maybe one day, Journey will release an official collection of alternate takes and unused demos.

Evolution (1979)

Personnel:
Steve Perry: lead vocals
Gregg Rolie: keyboards, lead vocals, vocals
Neal Schon: lead guitar, Roland GR-500 synthesizer guitar, vocals
Steve Smith: drums and percussion
Ross Valory: bass guitar, Moog bass, vocals
Produced by Roy Thomas Baker for RTB Audio-Visual Productions, Ltd. at Cherokee Studios, Los Angeles
Engineered by Geoffrey Workman and George Tutko
US release date: 20 March 1979
Highest chart position: US: 20; Certified 3x Platinum
Running time: 36:56

Evolution lived up to its name, not only in the changing nature of the songs but also in the major personnel change that happened. There are a few stories circulating about why the band changed drummers – any of them are plausible. The official word is that Aynsley Dunbar's drumming style simply wasn't a good fit. He played with John Mayall, David Bowie and Frank Zappa, among many others. As Journey turned toward pop rock and more lyrically focused music, would Dunbar be able to handle it? Given his later career with Jefferson Starship and Whitesnake, the answer is yes, but he would want to have his say. According to Dunbar, he was tired of being held back when playing live. Steve Perry, the emerging leader, wanted the live show to be as close to the studio work as possible. This frustrated the drummer. Schon stated: '(Dunbar) used to warm up during our songs for his drum solos.' Dunbar was fired, and according to some band members, it was a band decision.

In my opinion, the likely reason for his departure is a mix of his frustration with the music, the constraints on his live performance and his personality. He had led his own band, Retaliation, back in the 1960s, and he was vocal in his desire to avoid succumbing to the lure of balladeering. With Perry asserting himself and Herbie Herbert's big ego, there was little room for Dunbar to influence the musical direction. This had to be mutually frustrating. Given these conditions, his exit was inevitable.

There's a bit more to this story about Dunbar's shares in Nightmare. According to Golland, there were no legal grounds for firing Dunbar, and they couldn't simply force him to give up his shares in the company. Herbie created two new companies to spread the revenue. The live show production equipment and transportation services were moved to Nocturne, Inc., while the song royalties went to Daydream, Inc. This shift devalued Dunbar's shares in Nightmare, while his former bandmates were owners of the two new companies. In the first of Journey's many legal fights over the years, Nightmare settled with Dunbar for a quarter of a million dollars, and he gave up his shares in the company.

After leaving Journey, Dunbar's career was hardly over. He joined Jefferson Starship for two albums. To hear Dunbar's impact on the feel of a song, listen to 'Jane'. Later in the 1980s, Dunbar would work with David Coverdale and John Sykes on the iconic 1987 album *Whitesnake*, among others.

Journey answered the question of whom to bring on as a replacement during the 1978 tour. Steve Smith, the drummer for Montrose, impressed the group. Journey, likewise, impressed Smith. He came on board as a full member of the band and performed at their 1978 New Year's Eve show in San Francisco. Smith had been doing mostly session and touring work, such as that with Montrose, so this opportunity with Journey was his first full-time foray into being in a rock band. For good or ill, depending on your taste, his skill, varied musical experience and professionalism were major factors in Journey's development of a polished AOR sound.

They recorded *Evolution* in full at Cherokee Studios. They were not welcomed back at His Master's Wheels after the great fire extinguisher fight. Herbie and the band did not exactly want RTB at the console again either, but, per Herbie, they renegotiated a better deal with Columbia to let him produce once again. Luckily, Geoff Workman would again work the boards. Baker was rarely present, which suited the group just fine.

For this album, Perry received a writing credit on ten of the 11 tracks, including the two he wrote alone. He took an increasing share of the lead vocal duties, too, with Rolie singing lead on only one song. Still, Rolie's voice dominates the multitracked choruses, which is a key part of Journey's sound during this period.

Kelley and Mouse continue with their iconic wing motif around a central globe depicting a volcano seeping a river of lava. The band name is above the image and, unlike *Infinity* – where the title did not appear on the cover – *Evolution* is below. A group photo, with our first glimpse of Steve Smith, graces the reverse. The photo reflects the band's increased wardrobe budget. Ross Valory rocks a pale blue satin tuxedo with tails and a ruffled shirt, which was not an uncommon costume at the time for boys attending their high school proms.

'Majestic' (Schon, Perry) 1:15

This short instrumental starts with a pleasant phrase on acoustic guitar before the full band crash in on a minor chord. This repeats over several bars while Schon solos over the buildup. The tune continues to build into Perry's vocalese crescendo as Schon continues the guitar dramatics. The piece ends on a ten-second sustain. A recording of 'Majestic' was used to open concerts during the *Evolution* and *Departure* tours, complete with smoke and a stage rising from below. It was a simple and effective way to create crowd anticipation for the band's appearance. This would then be followed by a high-energy song such as 'Where Were You'. This track is collected on *Time*[3].

'Too Late' (Perry, Schon) 2:58

A bit of piano and guitar open this soulful song about a friend of Perry's who was battling addiction – a rare moment in which the band refrained from focusing on romantic relationships. The harmonies in the chorus help it soar. Schon keeps the guitar theatrics toned down at first before trying to match Perry's emotive power at the end of his solo. Perry delivers an emotional third verse: 'So my friend I join the fight for the things you know are right. Oh, you got to leave this town before it's too late'. The lyrics aren't poignant, but Perry's voice gives them weight and significance. I find it easy to get caught up in the moment when Perry turns up the volume.

This is a standout example of a finely crafted song from the Perry/Rolie years. 'Too Late' (with the B-side 'Do You Recall') charted in early 1980 and was the album's third single, reaching 70 on the *Billboard* Hot 100, where it lasted for a modest four weeks. The song is collected on *Time^3*.

'Lovin', Touchin', Squeezin'' (Perry) 3:50

Journey's first American top 40 hit is this Perry-penned slow jam with the unlikeliest of titles. Smith and Valory set the pace in one of Journey's most r&b-influenced songs ever. Based on Perry seeing a girlfriend kissing another guy, he wrote this as a revenge song, though he referred to it as 'love justice'. The song could not be simpler in construction, with piano and guitar over the top of that slow blues beat. The song is reminiscent of Sam Cooke's 'Nothing Can Change This Love' from 1963.

Perry's powerful voice fills the pocket created by Smith and Valory. At the 2:15 mark, Perry belts out, 'Now it's your turn girl to cry', and invites us to join in with the final two minutes of 'na, na, na, na, na' repeats. These chants swirl and build, the band adding their voices and Schon tearing through a solo throughout. It's an incredible mix of r&b and hard rock that really set Journey apart from their other arena rock contemporaries. The rhythm section are relentless in their groove, the piano spices it up and the guitar pyrotechnics supplement but don't overshadow the proceedings. The song ends in a dramatic smash cut like 'Feeling That Way'.

This was released as the second single from the album, with 'Daydream' on the B-side. It reached number 16 in October 1980 and was on the charts for 20 weeks. It is collected on *Greatest Hits*.

'City Of The Angels' (Perry, Rolie, Schon) 3:07

With 'Lights' rewritten to be about San Francisco, the band decided to write a new song about Los Angeles. Were they trying to recreate the dynamic magic of the 'Feeling That Way/Anytime' pairing from *Infinity*? Unlike 'Lights', this song is not really intended to be about LA. Rather, it is more about the feeling of being in LA and dreaming of success. It is a slight song, both lyrically and instrumentally. Schon's two solos are short and simple, and they move the music along without making a statement. The chorus sounds catchy enough to engage an audience in concert, but this song is rarely performed live.

'When You're Alone (It Ain't Easy)' (Perry, Schon) 3:09
Schon flexes his rhythm guitar muscles here with a crunchy intro. Perry sings one of his patented lonely guy songs. With lyrics including the title, the line 'ain't got nobody home' and repeated talk of teasing and being 'like a dog that roams', we are in shallow lyrical waters. Schon's lead guitar heats up a bit as the song zips along with a growing r&b flair. The song fades with Schon playing what sounds like a variation of Led Zeppelin's opening to 'Going To California'. It was released as the B-side to the lead single from *Departure*, 'Any Way You Want It'.

'Sweet And Simple' (Perry) 4:10
Another song that Perry brought with him when he joined Journey, he had written it at least five years earlier while admiring Lake Tahoe. If your Journey fandom was created in the pre-Perry era, then a song like this would likely drive you to distraction. Starting with a soulful piano with some guitar embellishments, we find ourselves in the middle of white soul territory. It's a beautiful song executed by a confident, mature band. The guitar solo is energetic while fitting neatly into its slow, rolling pace. For all the musicianship, it's the vocals that make this a great song. Perry sings with a heartfelt softness and then rapidly transforms into a powerful, soul-piercing gospel singer. At the 2:54 mark, after a beat of silence, everyone sings a soaring a cappella, 'It's what I like to do', which they repeat to the end, with Schon and Perry adding their respective ornamentation throughout. The song fades, 'sweet as sugar'. It's one of my favorites. This track is collected on *Time^3*.

'Lovin' You Is Easy' (Perry, Schon, Greg Errico) 3:36
Here we have a bubbly pop song, which has a cowriter in Sly & The Family Stone's and Mahavishnu Orchestra's drummer Greg Errico, who was part of Journey's early history (mentioned in the book's introduction). Opening like a rollicking hoedown, the verses are rowdy and punchy in contrast with the chorus, which stretches out the notes and is allowed to breathe. The melodic guitar solo leads to a bridge featuring the delicate tinkling of Rolie's piano before the final repeated chorus. The collective vocals of the band remain a strength in the final 'lovin' you is easy' repeats. The song zips along its well-crafted way to a guitar-driven fade-out. It was a concert mainstay until the *Frontiers* tour.

'Just The Same Way' (Rolie, Schon, Valory) 3:17
The eighth track is when we finally hear Rolie take the microphone, but it is well worth the wait. From the rolling piano intro to the opening line,

'Yesterday was a good day. It's after midnight and I've got you on my mind', Rolie sounds up for his moment. His voice is nowhere near the technical level of Perry's, but that hardly matters. Rolie has a unique, airy baritone, which is as instantly recognizable as Perry's massive tenor.

Here, Perry sings the response to Rolie's call during the chorus – Rolie: 'That's the same way she loves me'. Perry: 'That's the same way she loves you' – mirroring the live vocal interplay between the two singers during the early days of Perry being in the band, when set lists consisted of tracks from the first three albums. (You can find videos of these performances, which are great variations of the original songs.)

The band sing 'Oh, yeah' and 'Oh, no' before each line by Perry: 'You should be holding on to him, girl, just like, just like, you want to do. Just love and squeeze him girl. Just love and squeeze him yeah'. It's a superb moment in the live shows and on the album.

Barely over three minutes long and clearly intended for radio, this was the first song released from this album (b/w 'Somethin' To Hide') in the spring of 1979. It spent eight weeks on the *Billboard* Hot 100 and peaked at number 58. The song is collected on *Greatest Hits 2* and *Time*[3].

'Do You Recall' (Rolie, Perry) 3:12
'Do You Recall' served as the B-side to 'Too Late'. This is a rare Rolie-Perry collaboration, and surprisingly, it's a catchy pop song. As the band keeps repeating their three chords to a steady thumping beat, Perry gives another r&b-flecked performance. The chorus is especially singable: 'So you think that it's all over, and you know it's gone to stay. Oh, after stormy weather, does the sunshine every day?' Lyrically, there isn't much more to unpack, but the vocals from the band continue to emphasize their newfound radio-friendly chops. 'Do You Recall' is the last pop-rock song on the album. The final two cuts are decidedly different, with this track crossfading into 'Daydream'.

'Daydream' (Schon, Perry, Valory, Rolie) 4:40
Everyone but Steve Smith has songwriting credits on 'Daydream', and while it is more polished than most tracks on the first three albums, this song reflects the band's earlier style. It is, by far, the most complex song on *Evolution*, and it has the longest running time. The song opens with an ethereal wall of sound over a steady tempo. While Rolie plays keyboards, Schon is enjoying his new Roland GR-500 guitar synthesizer, which he uses at various times throughout the track.

While not a love song, Perry's interpretation remains soulful. A line such as 'Shining in the silver moon, crystal ships are sailing to the sea. Dreams the joys in pearls and gold, and our angel's wings in flight unfold' is perhaps one of Journey's most psychedelic. It sounds like we are on a completely different album, but they embrace the mood, keeping things airy and dreamlike.

Schon's guitar work is stellar throughout, and he's given the spotlight with a little over a minute left. As he finishes the solo, the opening wall of sound returns and takes the track to a well-earned fade.

'Lady Luck' (Perry, Valory, Schon) 3:34
The last track is the only true hard rock song on *Evolution*. Once again, we feel like we've left the album of the first nine tracks. We should note that this is the third song that Valory took part in as a writer, which will be a rare occurrence going forward. Rolie's Hammond B3 makes a welcome return, supplying a sonic shelter when these power chords come crashing down.

The song thunders, Rolie puts the B3 to work and Schon tears up the solo before the song concludes. The only drawback to this song is its short length. It could've benefitted from a longer instrumental section, allowing Rolie and Schon to trade riffs like old times. Given their improved arranging and compositional skills, this might have been a hard rock classic. For now, 'Lady Luck' is more of an out-of-place hard rock song on a mainstream pop rock album. Still, these last two tracks showed that Journey hadn't given up on their original sound, but it was only two songs. And they were edging closer to abandoning these sounds for quite a long time.

Related Tracks
'Good Times' (Cooke) 2:39
There were a variety of syndicated television and radio music programs during the 1970s and 1980s, and Herbie had Journey taking full advantage of them as part of his overall marketing plan. One of the popular radio shows was called *The King Biscuit Flower Hour*, which began airing on Sunday nights around the country in the winter of 1973. It was named in honor of an influential and long-running daily 30-minute live blues show, *King Biscuit Time*, which, in turn, was named for its sponsor, the King Biscuit Flour Company.

King Biscuit Flower Hour played recorded live music of various up-and-coming artists. Journey first appeared on the show on 28 May 1978 with a few songs from *Infinity*, *Next* and *Look Into The Future*, but only for half an hour. They shared the episode with Meat Loaf, whose album *Bat Out Of Hell* was storming the charts. Their second appearance on the program would be quite different. Recorded live in the studio in October 1978, this show was Steve Smith's performance debut with the band. He was still learning their songs.

Aired on 2 September 1979, the date of their final *Evolution* tour concert, the episode was called 'The Best Of The Biscuit – Superjam II' and it was fantastic. Freed of the constraints of being 'Journey' and with guest musicians working with them, they played a few of their own songs and then worked through selected covers. They were joined by Tom Johnston, guitarist and vocalist for The Doobie Brothers; two members of the California-based rock band Stoneground, Jo Baker and Annie Sampson; and the Tower of Power horn section. They recorded the session at the recently opened studio, The Automatt, in San Francisco.

The 12-song setlist begins with 'Feeling That Way' and 'Anytime' before they move to covers. The first cover is Junior Walker and the All-Stars' version of '(I'm A) Road Runner' before they perform Stoneground's choice of Nazareth's 'Love Hurts', featuring a cool moment by Perry in which he inserts a few lyrics from 'Unchained Melody'. Other songs include Sam & Dave's 'Hold On, I'm Coming', The Impressions' 'People Get Ready', Joe Tex's 'Show Me', Cream's 'Crossroads' and 'Born Under A Bad Sign' and – the track in question – Sam Cooke's 1964 hit 'Good Times'. The set ends with two more songs from *Infinity*, 'Lights' and 'Wheel In The Sky'.

'Good Times' opens with Perry counting everyone in, kickstarting a loping r&b shuffle. The song fits the mood; everyone is having a blast. Perry sings the chorus: 'Come on and let the good times roll. We going to stay until we soothe our soul if it takes all night long'. He sings 'soul' instead of 'souls', but no harm done.

The Tower of Power horns add depth and a range of tones that the Hammond couldn't provide. The trombone and bass saxophone notes at the end of the verses wouldn't be as emphatic on the synthesizer. Schon's tones harmonize well with the other brass and saxophones. I'd love to have heard Journey use more wind instruments in their rock songs. When they did use them, they would be included in larger arrangements that included strings.

'Good Times' is collected on *Time^3*. The other performances have not been officially released, but recordings are available on various sites such as YouTube and are worth searching for.

Departure (1980)

Personnel:
Steve Perry: lead vocals
Gregg Rolie: keyboards, harmonica, vocals
Neal Schon: guitars, vocals
Steve Smith: drums, percussion
Ross Valory: bass guitar, bass pedals, vocals
Produced by Geoff Workman and Kevin Elson at The Automatt, San Francisco
Engineered and mixed by Geoff Workman and Ken Kessie
Cover art: Kelley
Lettering: Mouse
US release date: 23 March 1980
Highest chart position: US: 8; Certified 3x Platinum
Running time: 37:55

Journey brought 19 songs to the San Francisco studio, The Automatt, in November 1979. Roy Thomas Baker was out, but Geoff Workman remained on board to produce. Sitting next to him was Journey's live sound engineer, Kevin Elson, earning his first producer credit. Workman did the engineering and left most of the production work to Elson.

Elson had been a roadie and sound engineer for Lynyrd Skynyrd and did critical work in the studio for *Street Survivors*. As a key member of the crew, he was aboard the ill-fated plane that left Greenville, South Carolina, on 20 October 1977. The plane ran out of fuel on its way to Baton Rouge, Louisiana, and crashed in the Mississippi woods, killing six people, including three band members. Elson and the other survivors sustained critical injuries.

Once able to work again, Elson became the live sound engineer during Journey's *Evolution* tour. The band, happy with his work on the road and Workman's in the studio, recorded *Departure* live in the studio. They limited the time-consuming construction of vocal tracks and doubling of instruments from the prior two albums, though some tracks did require extra sessions. Elson believed the drums and bass had been too subdued in the prior album's sound, something he wanted to improve for this album.

The band chose The Automatt because it was in San Francisco, near home, and they wanted a decent live space where they did not have to worry about scheduling, as was the case in Los Angeles at Cherokee Studios. The only equipment Elson brought in was some JBL studio monitors, which he preferred.

Of the 19 songs they had written while on the *Evolution* tour, where they also rehearsed them during sound checks, they recorded 14 of them and selected 11 for the album. The band came to the studio by 10 am and worked until three in the afternoon every day. According to Elson, if they didn't get a satisfactory track in the first two takes, they took a break or moved on to another song. It only took them two weeks to get the 14 songs recorded. According to Joel Selvin, nearly all of Perry's vocals are from the live recordings.

Departure hit the shelves in March 1980 and leaped up the charts to number eight, giving Journey their first *Billboard* top ten record. The album spent over a year on the *Billboard* Hot 200; however, *Infinity* and *Evolution* each spent twice as long on the charts. When *Departure* debuted on the charts, *Evolution* was still there, as was the quickly created 1979 'best of' compilation from the first three albums, *In The Beginning*, giving Journey three simultaneously charting records.

The *Departure* tour kicked off at home in San Francisco on 26 March 1980. They stayed on the road in North America until the Chicago performance on 1 September. They toured Europe in September with dates in Germany and Switzerland and a last show on 22 September in London. The last leg of this tour took them to Japan for a show in Osaka and three in Tokyo. They would stay in Japan for a special one-off project, *Dream, After Dream*, which is covered after *Departure*.

Once again, Kelley did the cover art, and Mouse did the lettering. *Departure* is the first album to feature the scarab, taken from the duo's 1970 work on an unreleased album cover for Jimi Hendrix. The band loved the scarab image, and Kelley depicted the beetle flying between a blue planet and its moon. The planet has a golden torus orbit, as in the two earlier albums. A neon rainbow of parallel borders surrounds the image, and the Journey name is cut out on all four sides. The graphics have a neon 1980s vibe, as do the soft-focused black and white portraits of the band on the back cover. The album sleeve features a color band photo of them standing on a highway overpass near San Francisco. They look chilled, but again, their wardrobe budget continues to show improvement. Neal Schon's spouse, Tena Austin, received credit for doing their makeup.

It's a dark and weirdly claustrophobic album package. It matches the music, which is not as sunny and bright as *Evolution*, but shows the band willing to take some chances and not just fill out the record with radio-ready tunes. The live-in-studio recording does give the faster rock songs ('Any Way You Want It', 'Where Were You' and 'Line Of Fire') a sense of momentum.

'Any Way You Want It' (Perry, Schon) 3:21
The first track, also the first single, was released three weeks before the album proper (with the B-side 'When You're Alone (It Ain't Easy)' from *Evolution*). 'Any Way You Want It', per Schon and Perry, was inspired by Phil Lynott. Thin Lizzy and Journey shared the road from mid-June through August 1979. They liked the vocal/guitar interplay that you hear in songs like the similarly named 'Do Anything You Want To Do' from *Black Rose: A Rock Legend*.

One of Journey's most up-tempo tracks, it starts with the band singing the chorus – 'Any way you want it, that's the way you need it, any way you want it' – and it does not let up for the next three minutes. Perry delivers each line of the verses with space for Schon's rhythm guitar in the gaps. We hear a 15-second preview guitar solo around the 1:30 mark. Then, two minutes into the song, Schon delivers a searing solo, starting off melodic, copying the notes from the chorus, which join in over the guitar. This allows Schon to climb higher up the neck and creates a powerful resolution to the song as it fades.

The *Time³* liner notes discuss the double-tracking of Rolie's Mellotron and the Hammond B3. The Mellotron is often used to provide breathy, sustained notes in a variety of tones, most famously on the opening to The Beatles' 'Strawberry Fields Forever' or with the opening guitar on David Bowie's 'Space Oddity'. Rolie's keyboards provide support to the backing vocals, giving them texture and depth. The double-tracking was required because the Mellotron was not working as planned, so Workman had him record it on the B3, and this doubled keyboard is what we hear.

This is the first song by Journey that found its way onto a movie soundtrack. *Caddyshack* hit the cinemas in the summer of 1980. A silly Harold Ramis golf comedy, it features a scene with Rodney Dangerfield cranking up a stereo installed in his golf bag. He and other golfers dance to a blaring 'Any Way You Want It'. *Charlie's Angels: Full Throttle*, from 2003, used it as the music over the gag reel scenes in the closing credits. Among other uses, the song was the core concept in an amusing State Farm Insurance commercial where the customer and the agent had 'a little Journey moment' with the song's lyrics.

This classic hit the *Billboard* Hot 100 on 1 March 1980, lasting 15 weeks and peaking at 23. The track is collected on *Time³* and *Greatest Hits*.

'Walks Like A Lady' (Perry) 3:16
The second track, also the second single, is this low-key blues tune from Perry. Rolie's B3 starts the proceedings with Valory laying down a stuttering bass line, Smith adding a cool brushed beat and Schon plucking away at the Stratocaster in a tight performance. It's an infectious blues-pop song from a band experimenting with different approaches to songwriting while not straying too far from commercial appeal. The song charted on 24 May 1980 (with the B-side 'People And Places'), staying on for 13 weeks and peaking during the summer at number 32. The track is collected on *Greatest Hits 2*.

'Someday Soon' (Perry, Rolie, Schon) 3:31
This is only one of two songs co-written by Gregg Rolie on *Departure* and the only one to feature Rolie on lead vocals. This is a throwback to the pre-Perry songs but with better songwriting, a fine arrangement and a more focused musicality. These are the types of songs that will be sorely missed by older Journey fans like me after Rolie's exit.

The slow beat and guitar textures evoke the dreamier tracks from the debut album. Instead of being buried under layers of guitar and thundering drums, Rolie's singing is clear and forward. Perry remains restrained in the verses in order to allow Rolie his moment.

This song is collected on *Time*[3], where the liner notes quote Rolie's story of a college writing to them to say that they 'used this song in a music composition class as an example of good writing structure.'

'People And Places' (Perry, Schon, Valory) 5:04

If 'Someday Soon' made you think fondly about Journey's early days, then you will enjoy 'People And Places'. This is the last song during the Perry era that has neither a hint of r&b nor a soft rock ballad sensibility, nor is it driven by a Schon riff, making it nearly unique in their catalog. Dominated by synthesizers, including Valory on rumbling bass pedals, this is the second song on the album with shared lead vocals. This time, Schon joins Perry on the mic, opening the song with multiple backing vocalists repeating each word in the line 'Do you feel me?'

The lyrics are a throwback to those generic, vague sentiments from the pre-Perry days. In response to Schon's questions about seeing faces and whether these people are worth knowing, Perry sings his heartfelt reply. Yes, he has seen them, and in 'every single face, there lies a trace of sadness felt before'. The song gives off a melancholy vibe but feels empathetic. This whole sequence repeats, but this time, Schon declares that 'you're the people that we want to know' and Perry belts out a positive message about thinking differently, protecting yourself and trying to get where you need to go despite the sadness. Once Jonathan Cain joined the band, optimistic songs became a staple on Journey albums.

Schon's repeated five-note phrase at the end of the bridge is one of those subtle moments, in addition to his solo a few seconds later, that add heft. The song fades to a gentle synthesizer finish. 'People And Places' is the longest song on *Departure*. Played occasionally during the next tour, this is one of my favorite Journey songs.

'Precious Time' (Perry, Schon) 4:48

Opening with a jangly rhythm guitar, this shuffle evokes a train rumbling down the tracks, an effect enhanced by Rolie's harmonica, which joins shortly after the first verse. The rhythm section doesn't join until the 1:20 mark. This is a rock song that has some elements of, but never quite slips into, a blues rock groove. Perry sells the lyrics, even when they make little sense. This is an easy one to sing along with and it has satisfying moments. It's another personal favorite of mine, and it is an excellent way to end side one.

'Where Were You' (Perry, Schon) 2:59

Most melodic rock albums begin with a solo guitar riff for a couple of bars, and this is no exception, with this intro bringing to mind Motley Crüe's 1983 song 'Looks That Kill'. In terms of subject matter, there isn't much to it, apart from the repeated chant of the song title in the chorus, rendering this as a boring example of generic pop rock. This three-minute gap filler opens side two. The song was developed during a jam session in Oakland. Schon said it was influenced by one of the concert tour's opening acts: AC/DC. However, it lacks the four-on-the-floor march of most AC/DC songs. Still, this was a favorite opener for the band during their run at the top. For me, it is easily the least inspired song on *Departure*. This track is collected on *Time³*.

'I'm Cryin'' (Perry, Rolie) 3:42
A second collaboration between Perry and Rolie opens with a slow blues beat in E minor, and Schon sounds much more comfortable soloing in the gaps between Perry's powerful performance. It opens on a cymbal crash, with Schon playing atop an atmospheric interplay between bass and piano. The 50-second intro sets up a dramatic moment for Perry's vocals. Rolie switches to the organ, which undergirds the dramatics. Schon's solos and flourishes only get better.

'Line Of Fire' (Perry, Schon) 3:04
'Line Of Fire' is about Frankie threatening Suzie with a shotgun for cheating on Stevie. Why is Frankie shouldering this 'love justice' burden? Where is Stevie during the song? Does Stevie even care? The lyrics are ridiculous, exemplified by lines like, 'standing in the line of fire it's gonna shoot ya'. Topping off the shenanigans is a recording of a shotgun blast, which Elson and Workman had to insert mid-song. We do not know if Frankie killed Suzie or if he fired a warning shot, then dropped the gun and ran.

Despite the silly lyrics, this is a solid boogie rocker with the guitar delivering the energy. The guitar solo, starting around the midpoint, is an album highlight and takes us right up to the shotgun blast. 'Line Of Fire' remains popular in concert. This song is the B-side of the 'Good Morning Girl/Stay Awhile' single and is on *Time³*.

'Departure' (Schon) 0:38
Returning to having a title track after not doing so on *Infinity* and *Evolution*, the band chose Schon's half-minute ethereal guitar exercise. 'Departure' slows down the heart rate after 'Line Of Fire' and prepares the listener for two of the most mellow tracks Journey would put on any album.

'Good Morning Girl' (Perry, Schon) 1:43
This gorgeous little tune continues Schon's soft guitar tones from 'Departure'. Rolie's synthesized strings make this sound like one of Schubert's Lieder. According to the *Time³* liner notes, Neal's father, Matthew Schon, helped with the arrangement. The song has no chorus and no rhythm section. Perry's voice wrings passion from the simple lyrics. It's a touching love song ready-made for weddings. This, along with the next track, 'Stay Awhile', formed the third single released from this album (with the B-side 'Line Of Fire'), peaking at number 55 at the end of the summer of 1980 and staying on the charts for

a modest eight weeks. The two songs are collected on *Greatest Hits 2*, while this track made it on *Time³*.

'Stay Awhile' (Perry, Schon) 2:46

The second half of the third single is this soulful slow jam. The rhythm section are back, and over their steady pocket, we have guitar and piano figures setting up Perry. His vocals are made to deliver these quietly intense verses, which lead to a soaring chorus aided by excellent backing vocals and Rolie's lush string synthesizers. While Perry's big notes tend to get the attention, sometimes it's the little touches that make the difference. When he sings at the end of the second verse, 'ooh, I'd do all this and so much more', he adds a syllable, turning 'more' into 'mo-ah', an embellishment that makes the song his. There is a similar example we will hear later during 'Who's Crying Now'. As said above, this is part of the third single from *Departure* and this track is collected on *Greatest Hits 2*.

'Homemade Love' (Perry, Schon, Smith) 2:52

Steve Smith makes his first appearance as a songwriter and his influence on the stuttering shuffle is clear from the outset. Schon repeats a five-note phrase throughout the verses. Perry's voice is too smooth and round for the atmosphere this song requires. The references to 'hot jelly roll love' do not work, no matter how much high-note scatting Perry can muster. It's all quite awkward. *AllMusic* called this 'a weak attempt to boogie that falls absolutely flat', while *Ultimate Classic Rock* described it as 'sludgy (and) clumsily salacious.' I agree. 'Homemade Love' is collected on *Time³*.

Related Tracks
'Natural Thing' (Perry, Valory) 3:41

Poor Ross Valory – here we have another song of his that didn't make it onto a studio album (see 'Cookie Duster' on *Next*.) This co-write with Steve Perry deserved to be included, but the consolation prize as the B-side to 'Don't Stop Believin'' in 1981 was pretty good. The track is also on *Time³*. Recorded during the *Departure* sessions, the song was considered a superfluous r&b-influenced song for an album that already had a couple of them. I would have put it in over 'Homemade Love', but Valory had a song credit with 'People And Places', so perhaps Smith's contribution was chosen for balance.

The few Valory-penned songs tend to have a thoughtful, melodic piano introduction, as we have here. After that, we step into a slow r&b beat, and Perry's lyrics and voice shine in all their melancholy power. Love with 'Julie' has gone – 'it's a natural thing'. With piano support throughout and Schon's soulful 20-second solo at the 2:20 mark, we have, in my opinion, a classic. This is Journey doing their finest white soul.

Dream, After Dream (1980)

Personnel:
Steve Perry: lead and backing vocals
Gregg Rolie: keyboards, harmonica
Neal Schon: guitars, vocals
Steve Smith: drums, percussion
Ross Valory: bass, piano, recorder
Produced by Kevin Elson and Journey
Recorded at CBS Sony Shinamonachi Studios, Tokyo
Engineered and mixed by Kevin Elson
Engineers: Akira Fukada, Knichi Yoshimura
Strings and brass arranged and conducted by Matthew Schon
Release date: 10 December 1980 (Japan)
Highest chart position: US: did not chart
Running time: 35:22

The world tour supporting *Departure* ended on 13 October 1980 in Tokyo, Japan. Instead of heading home after the long months of touring, Journey headed into CBS Sony's Shinamonachi Studios to spend the next week recording a soundtrack album for the movie *Yume, Yume, No Ato* or *Dream, After Dream*. How did this happen? Why would a musical group, riding high on three hit albums, take time out to record a couple of songs and some incidental music for a Japanese art house movie?

The story begins during the *Evolution* tour, which opened with five shows in Japan in April 1979. The concerts were sparsely attended, including one Tokyo show that housed less than 200 people. Across town, Boston filled Nippon Budokan that same night on their *Don't Look Back* tour. This embarrassment for the Japanese promoters had to be remedied. Journey returned for multiple dates in 1980 (though notably not yet at the Budokan) to crowds of 2,000 or more.

In addition to better-attended shows, the band were asked to record music for a new movie – directed and co-written by France-based Japanese fashion designer – Kenzo Takada, which was released in January 1981. Takada envisioned music from the first version of Santana, a band lineup that no longer existed. But the next best thing was available with Neal Schon and Gregg Rolie, and they were going to be in Tokyo in October. Agreements were settled and Journey entered the studio with their sound engineer and budding producer, Kevin Elson. They would be joined by a 30-piece orchestra, with arrangements and orchestrations by Matthew Schon.

Over the following week, they recorded a Journey album like no other. Initially released only in Japan in December 1980, the album had three tracks featuring vocals, and Perry sings in a noticeably lower register; of course, he had recently finished a long world tour. Clearly, the music was not intended for commercial release, as exemplified by some of the sublime and spellbinding musical moments on offer. The album should be a treat for Journey fans. While, for years, this was only available as an import, a US release finally happened, though you won't find this on all streaming services.

The movie did not fare well. In France, critics panned it, and Takada removed it from distribution. No showings, home video releases, or streaming of the film have happened since that time, which is unfortunate. How fascinating would it be to see this music with the images it was intended to support?

The album cover art shows swans taking flight high above a desert oasis and a sandcastle. The concept was created by Takada and Aki Morishita, and it does evoke a dreamlike state. The gatefold includes stills from the movie. There is an amusing band photo featuring a couple of doves. An informative insert (in Japanese) helps put the music in context.

'Destiny' (Schon, Perry) 8:55
The movie's primary theme opens with a quiet guitar melody over a bed of synthesized strings. At 1:50, Perry identifies the characters in the film – 'a lonely boy and two lonely girls' – who set out to find riches and heartbreak in this exotic setting. He flexes his vocal powers but keeps it low-key. The band's mystical backing vocals on the 'fly away' repeats continue the relaxed mood of the track.

Around the 4:40 mark, strings (violins, violas and cellos) join the guitar as Schon builds speed and dynamics, leading to an extended instrumental section that shatters the established mellow mood. At the five-minute mark, Smith and Valory join in. This throwback segment rollicks along for the next minute and a half, sounding like Journey's pre-Perry days. The boys are enjoying this old-school section.

As this ends, Schon continues playing over strings and acoustic guitar. The drums and bass rejoin for this extended guitar solo, which concludes at 8:05. Then, Rolie steps in to play some spacey chords on the electric piano – sounding like an experimental classical composition – to take it the rest of the way.

This, not 'Look Into The Future', is their longest studio track. It has enjoyable musical moments and feels like something from their early albums.

'Snow Theme' (Valory) 3:24
This charming instrumental track is a rarity because it features no guitar, drums or bass. We have the string orchestra – conducted by Matthew Schon – and Ross Valory on piano. It opens with the strings playing twice through a slow melody in F minor with piano accompaniment. The strings stop to let Valory play a quiet, contemplative piano section that is more mood than melody. The strings return with the opening theme, but this time with the cellos and double basses adding a new line underneath. After the repeat,

Valory's piano repeats its section, but slightly faster this time, before slowing down to allow the strings to return for one final repeat of the main theme. The double basses and cellos bring this to a close over sustained notes from the violas and violins. The piano joins for one final melancholy moment.

'Sandcastles' (Rolie, Perry) 4:42
The third and final collaboration from Rolie and Perry is a moody track in C minor. With a slow, stumbling beat and light guitar, Rolie's keyboard is joined by the strings to give us a dreamy foundation for Perry to deliver some atmospheric crescendos. The words stay simple ('sunrise and dreams'), showing the desert castle setting of the movie. We also hear another rarity on a Journey track: saxophone. Takeshi Ito, at the time the flute and alto sax player in The Square, showcases some extended solos. He is still an active jazz musician, and his presence here adds aural complexity to the ethereal sounds. Listen closely to Steve Smith having some fun on the drums.

'A Few Coins' (Rolie, Schon, Smith, Perry, Valory) 0:42
The entire band get credit for writing this little filler piece, which is a few guitar chords accompanied by a couple of synthesizer tones.

'Moon Theme' (Schon, Perry) 4:36
This opens like a well-produced track from *Next* or *Journey*. Schon plays the melody doubled by the string orchestra. It makes for a lovely opening minute. The rhythm section joins, and Schon plays a rising figure that, with the supporting strings, sounds downright exultant. This lasts for half a minute before returning to the opening melody. At the 3:20 mark, we hit the final 30-second triumphal strings and guitar section. This fades, and we hear a harp solo played by Keiko Yamakawa, which takes us to the end of the piece.

'When The Love Has Gone' (Schon) 4:02
Foreshadowing Schon's later solo work, 'When The Love Has Gone' is an excellent slow-burn rock guitar workout. Lightly accompanied by drums, bass and keyboard, he plays an extended solo that suggests the best work of Steve Vai or Joe Satriani. Enthusiasts of the soulful tracks from these guitar heroes will find lots to love here. This deserves to be included on their concert set lists, perhaps as part of Schon's solo time.

'Festival Dance' (Rolie, Schon, Smith, Perry, Valory) 0:59
Another short filler that is attributed to the entire band. Intended to sound like a Moroccan celebration, it's more like five guys trying to sound exotic with handclaps and drums at a local bazaar. It goes on for 45 seconds before a pause, and then an electronic cacophony, akin to a bomb going off, hits in the last ten seconds. This odd track disrupts the flow of the album.

'The Rape' (Valory, Perry) 2:12
Matthew Schon's string orchestra opens in a romantic swirl, joined by the horns before settling down into an extended section that could have been lifted straight from the Tatooine scenes in *Star Wars*. Here, Smith taps a deliberate beat on what sounds like a tubular bell while the woodwinds take up a slow, repetitive dirge. The first section does not match the piece's title, leading the listener to believe that we have an onscreen scene of innocent love that devolves into a crime. The brooding sounds lengthen and deepen into a howling lamentation in the final half minute, with the bell continuing its relentless clang. It's a sad downer of a track after such a bright beginning, with the contrast making it even more effective.

'Little Girl' (Schon, Perry, Rolie) 5:50
This song was recorded during the *Departure* sessions and, in keeping with an album stuffed full of minor key music, was brought into the *Dream, After Dream* session for a string arrangement to be added. While it doesn't quite fit with the overall vibe of the soundtrack, the band worked this into one of the finer tracks of the Rolie era.

The 30-second intro by the Schon duo of string orchestra and acoustic guitar is something I wish they would have pursued more on future albums. I would have welcomed an extended intro or a longer standalone prelude to the main song. Perry sings the verses with a quiet gravitas, along with the strings and guitar. By the second verse, the bass joins in, and as Perry's singing builds to the chorus, the drums arrive to create the feel of a slow rock song. The chorus, a repeated 'ooh, little girl', lacks fire when contrasted with the verses. The lyrics leading to the bridge are also lackluster, but that is soon forgotten when Schon starts his solo, which continues for well over a minute before returning to the chorus. Once the vocals peak and fade, we are treated to a final minute of Schon's acoustic guitar, Perry's haunting vocalese and some fine nostalgic harmonica from Rolie, who makes his final appearance on a Journey studio album.

'Little Girl' found its way onto *Departure* as a bonus track on the CD release and is collected on both *Greatest Hits 2* and *Time^3*. It was also the B-side to the big hit from *Escape*, 'Open Arms'.

Captured (1981)

Personnel:
Neal Schon: guitars, backing vocals
Ross Valory: bass, backing vocals
Steve Smith: drums, percussion
Steve Perry: lead and backing vocals
Gregg Rolie: keyboards, lead and backing vocals
Steve 'Keys' Roseman: keyboards on 'The Party's Over (Hopelessly In Love)'
Produced and engineered by Kevin Elson
Remixed by Rodney Mills and Kevin Elson at Studio One, Doraville, Georgia
US release date: 30 January 1981
Highest chart position: US: 9; 2x Platinum Certified
Running time: 1:11:18

Part of Herbie's plans all along, the live album *Captured* was recorded during the *Departure* tour and ready for release early in 1981. Kevin Elson, who coproduced *Departure* with Geoff Workman, had already served as their live engineer for the past two tours and produced *Dream, After Dream*. Given this record of accomplishment, he was the obvious choice for producing and remixing the live album.

Captured was the final official album to feature Gregg Rolie. After years of touring and recording with Santana and Journey, he was ready to leave the road and rockstar life and start a family, which is what he did. However, he did return to the studio for some solo work throughout the 1980s and formed The Storm in the early 1990s.

Captured is a collection of recordings from at least four different shows, including Montreal, Tokyo, and two dates in Detroit. Journey, like many aging melodic rock bands, have released many live albums and videos over the years, usually to help promote a tour or as fan service for new content. However, because *Captured* was always a step in the grand plan, we will cover the tracks in some detail. The album does have two new songs: 'Dixie Highway', written on the road and referring to what is now mostly Interstate-75 and US-25, and 'The Party's Over (Hopelessly In Love)', which serves as the obligatory studio cut to entice reluctant fans to buy a double live album.

The cover features art by Mouse, who, up to this point, had only been supplying the lettering for Journey albums. The winged scarab is enclosed in a circle, which encloses another smaller scarab in a circle – this continues indefinitely.

'Majestic' (Schon, Perry) 0:40
A recording of this opened each concert as the band took the stage. The crowd cheer, and as 'Majestic' nears its end, Steve Perry grabs the microphone and yells, 'Bonsoir, Montréal!'

'Where Were You' (Perry, Schon) 3:21
The band kick off the live show with a high-energy take of this song from *Departure*. There's an extended opening with Perry in fine form.

'Just The Same Way' (Rolie, Schon, Valory) 3:36
They roll directly into this track from *Evolution*, with Rolie sharing vocals with Perry. Rolie sounds confident, the piano is well-mixed and the song is played with slightly more energy than the studio cut. It is tough to find fault with Journey as a live act. Schon rips through his solo practically note-for-note from the studio version before his final embellishments extend the song for 20 seconds or so.

'Line Of Fire' (Perry, Schon) 3:17
The last of the opening trio of rockers comes from *Departure*. Steve Smith and Neal Schon are standouts on the pulse-pounding track, with Smith providing (or enhancing) the shotgun blast effect on percussion. This is the final track taken from the 8 August 1980 Montreal show.

'Lights' (Perry, Schon) 3:30
Perry tells the crowd that this song is about their hometown of San Francisco. The collective vocals are not as powerful as the studio overdubs, but the chorus sounds fine here. Schon's solo is tasteful and wanders off the studio path as the song transitions directly into the next track. Both this song and the next are collected on *Time³*. This collected version of 'Lights' also charted in 1993, peaking at 30 on the *Billboard* Adult Contemporary chart.

'Stay Awhile' (Perry, Schon) 2:17
Perry at once launches into this shortened version of the hit song from *Departure*. He embellishes his studio pronunciation of 'more', making it sound like it's a two-syllable word. 'Lights' and 'Stay Awhile' are from the final show of the tour on 13 October 1980, which took place in Tokyo.

'Too Late' (Perry, Schon) 3:40
The rest of *Captured* was recorded over two shows at Cobo Hall in Detroit, Michigan. The band had already performed five shows in Detroit in May 1980. These final two shows were on 4 and 5 August.
  Perry gets the crowd going by pointing out the microphones and explaining that they are part of the recording of a live album. Like a good crowd, they give a hearty response, and Journey kick off a by-the-numbers rendition of 'Too Late' from *Evolution*.

'Dixie Highway' (Perry, Schon) 6:52
Our first original song comes in the form of this southern fried rocker, which, according to Perry, is about 'a highway that runs from Detroit all the way

down to Florida, the Dixie Highway', also known as Interstate-75. Perry liked the term 'Dixie Highway', and the band developed the song during rides on the tour bus. 'Dixie Highway' has only been released as a live cut.

The extended intro features Rolie on synthesizer before a rapid buildup by the rhythm section. Schon delivers a series of flourishes – reminding me of Bachman-Turner Overdrive, like 'Roll On Down The Highway' or 'You Ain't Seen Nothing Yet' – over a high-tempo shuffle.

When they downshift to the bridge, Rolie has switched over to the Hammond B3 and the band engage in a classic rocking blues jam. Schon lets fly with a searing solo, and Steve Smith has never sounded more like a pure rock drummer than he does here. It's as if Journey decided to cover a Molly Hatchet song. It's a fun and welcome break from the regular catalog. The song spent one week at number 30 on the *Billboard* Mainstream Rock Airplay chart and is collected on *Time*[3].

'Feeling That Way' (Perry, Rolie, Dunbar) 3:13
Rolie starts off an up-tempo and slightly awkward version of 'Feeling That Way' from *Infinity*. It all sounds rushed, from the opening piano to Rolie's and Perry's vocals.

'Anytime' (Rolie, Silver, Fleischman, Schon, Valory) 4:24
The lore of Journey fandom says that 'Anytime' must follow 'Feeling That Way', or we risk disrupting the musical space-time continuum. Thankfully, Journey keep the musical multiverse intact with an energetic take on this classic. 'Anytime' is a product of the studio, with the producer, Roy Thomas Baker, stacking vocals on top of vocals, but the band do an admirable job of emulating that sound on stage. Rolie seems to relish his chance to lead the charge here, and the band sound confident, feeding off the energy from the crowd, especially when compared to 'Feeling That Way'.

The studio cut has a muscular instrumental section to conclude the song. Here, Perry calls out to the fans in Cobo Hall, 'Yeah, I'm talking to you, Detroit.' He improvises during the gaps in the chorus when the band shift gears. Rolie hammers staccato chords on the piano, and Perry sings about Detroit city. The chorus of 'woo, woo, woo, anytime that you want me' returns in a hyper-speed boogie. With less than a minute to go at this new tempo, Schon plays a scorching solo. By the end, 'Anytime' has become a rowdy boogie stomper, with Smith's fills building momentum. When the band end the song with an emphatic 'anytime you want it', the crowd roar their appreciation.

Rarely do Journey turn their hits into something new and exciting as they do here and on 'Walks Like A Lady' (see below). As they reach the peak of their popularity over the next few albums, it will happen even less often during their live shows. Another Journey live album, *Live In Japan 2017*, has another example of this approach on 'Mother, Father'.

'Do You Recall' (Rolie, Perry) 3:21
I make no bones about this little pop tune being one of my favorite songs. I enjoy a simple melody, bright, upbeat lyrics, excellent guitar work and great singing. I prefer the studio version, but this works fine live.

'Walks Like A Lady' (Perry) 7:06
Tracks like this are why I love live albums: taking a song and stretching it out, flexing some musical muscles and letting the crowd hear what you can do. On *Departure*, 'Walks Like A Lady' is barely a three-minute song. Perry lets everyone know that Schon, on his Stratocaster, and Rolie, on his Hammond B3, will lead the proceedings as 'two of the best blues players in the whole world.' Over Valory and Smith, Schon and Rolie trade some simple phrases before Perry joins in with some scatting and then wailing, 'She's a cry cry baby'.

The song proper starts around the 1:50 mark. As you listen, you anticipate that they are going to improvise. After a solid bridge, they return to the chorus and repeat it over a sonic bed of Rolie's Hammond before Schon plays a second solo. Perry sings a variation of the chorus to bring it to a powerful conclusion, repeating, 'She's a cry cry baby'.

Schon continues the track with his minute-long guitar solo, inspired by Van Halen's 'Eruption' and ending with a lot of whammy bar. If you were wondering where the unlabeled guitar solo is on *Captured*, it's at the end of 'Walks Like A Lady'. This song, including the solo, is collected on *Time³*.

'La Do Da' (Perry, Schon) 7:06
The final sounds of the guitar solo stretch directly into 'La Do Da', which is an unapologetic guitar-driven rocker. Smith gets to demonstrate that he is a worthy successor to Dunbar; he was sometimes discussed as a 'jazz drummer', but as a *Rolling Stone* review of *Departure* said, '(Smith's) steady, unspectacular drumming has proved to be an addition by subtraction' when compared with Dunbar's 'virtuosic' style.

During an extended bridge, around the 3:00 mark, Valory plays some bass runs accompanied by Smith. At 4:00, Smith begins his drum solo for the next 1:45. After a short ten-second break, he continues his solo for nearly another minute. Perry gives him the nickname 'Steve 'Machine Gun' Smith' as his solo ends, which feels well-earned.

'Lovin', Touchin', Squeezin'' (Perry) 5:09
Steve Perry opens this with a little pandering lead singer talk: 'How about if we do the rest of the tour with you? We'll take you on buses across the country. Does that sound good?' As they cheer in response, the band crank up Journey's biggest hit to date. Apart from an extended guitar solo and far fewer 'na na na' lines, this is a tame version. The band do not give the fans a chance to sing on their own, which a hit like this seems tailor-made to do. This version is collected on *Time³*.

'Wheel In The Sky' (Schon, Fleischman, D. Valory) 5:00

Saving the big hits for the end of the setlist, this first hit for Journey sounds great live. The faster tempo and brighter mix would have served the original well. The vocals sound much better here than on *Infinity*. This version would have made a fine single. Smith seems to sound better as this album goes on. Finally, the band let the crowd have a moment to perform as they belt out 'For tomorrow' directly before the bridge. This is collected on *Time^3*.

'Any Way You Want It' (Perry, Schon) 3:39

Journey plunge into their latest hit from *Departure* to end the live part of the album. An already high-energy song gets revved up here, and Perry lets the Detroit crowd join in with call-and-response repeats of 'All night' and 'Hold tight'. Schon shreds throughout, and the band build to the big rock finish without overextending the tune. This track is as enjoyable as the studio cut. It is a fine way to end the show.

'The Party's Over (Hopelessly In Love)' (Perry) 3:42

Perry wrote the song while backstage in Detroit during the tour. He was noodling on the bass, according to the *Time^3* liner notes, and the band played the tune during sound checks.

After the tour and the *Dream, After Dream* session, Journey entered Fantasy Studios in Berkeley, California, to record it for inclusion on *Captured*. Adding a studio track was a customary practice to help drive an increase in album sales. However, the band no longer had a keyboard player. Gregg Rolie moved on after the soundtrack was recorded. The piano and keyboard parts would be recorded by new band member Jonathan Cain, except he wasn't available. This situation led to a classic question of Journey trivia: Who was the keyboardist between Gregg Rolie and Jonathan Cain? The answer is Stevie 'Keys' Roseman, a session musician who played piano and synthesizer on this song. Another bit of Journey trivia is that Roseman would go on to form the band VTR with Ross Valory and George Tickner in 2004, releasing one album, *Cinema*, in 2005.

The song tends to hold a special place for long-time Journey fans because it was the one new thing between *Departure* and *Escape* and we all hungered for content.

For a Perry solo composition, it rocks more than expected. The lyrical content about him being ghosted by a girlfriend is not unusual territory for Perry. But for me, I love the ambiguity of the repeated line in the song's second half: 'The party's over. I have gone away'. On the surface, it makes the guy look tough; he doesn't need her, and he's moved on. But the sheer amount of repetition introduces doubt, at least for me. Why does this guy need to keep saying this? In that regard, it's a clever pop song. Schon's guitar parts are reminiscent of another song I enjoyed back then, Donnie Iris's 'Ah, Leah'.

'The Party's Over (Hopelessly In Love)' was the only single released from *Captured* (with the B-side 'Just The Same Way' (live version)), which peaked at number 34 in April 1981 and stayed on the *Billboard* Hot 100 for 13 weeks. It also charted at number two on the Mainstream Rock Airplay chart, spending ten weeks there. The song is collected on *Greatest Hits 2* and *Time^3*. For the curious, it was also used on the soundtrack for the 2010 Adam Sandler movie *Grown Ups*.

Escape (1981)

Personnel:
Jonathan Cain: keyboards, vocals
Steve Perry: lead vocals
Neal Schon: guitars, vocals
Steve Smith: drums, percussion
Ross Valory: bass guitar, vocals
Produced by Mike Stone and Kevin Elson
Recorded and mixed at Fantasy Studios, Berkeley, California
Assistant Engineer: Wally Buck
US release date: 31 July 1981
Highest chart position: US: 1; Diamond Certified (10x Platinum)
Running time: 42:39

The Babys opened for Journey for significant parts of the *Departure* tour. Behind the scenes, though, The Babys were a financial mess, and their lead singer and leader, John Waite, was ready to launch a solo career. Meanwhile, Gregg Rolie had announced he was leaving Journey. Regardless of the status of The Babys, Herbie and Journey set their sights on hiring their keyboardist, Jonathan Cain. For his part, Cain disbelieved that they were interested but was willing to take advantage of the opportunity. To his surprise, they structured the deal to make him a full one-sixth member of the band, working his way to a full share over three years while Rolie's share diminished over that time. Cain flew to northern California to meet the band and begin rehearsals.

By this point, Steve Perry was in charge of the music. He and Schon had formed a solid songwriting team. Meanwhile, Cain continued his maturation as a composer, learning a great deal while working with John Waite. Cain had some specific principles in mind when it came to a song's subject matter. He told his new bandmates, 'You need to write songs about your fans and to your fans, and they have to be from the heart.' When it comes to earnestness, as we will see in some of his treaclier lyrics, Cain is a master.

Cain's influence was immediate, and from *Escape* onwards, his presence looms on each record. His approach to songwriting has shaped the sound of Journey. His effect on Journey's sound is as important as Steve Perry's voice and Neal Schon's guitar. Yet here we are on their tenth official release (not counting *In The Beginning*), so how can we say how important his impact has been? The re-release of *Greatest Hits* has 16 tracks; Cain wrote or co-wrote 12 of them. That's significant output for a songwriter who only appeared on four albums represented in that seminal collection.

Geoff Workman, who had engineered or produced the last three main studio albums, had moved on. Kevin Elson would be sitting at the console, this time beside long-time engineer and protégé of Roy Thomas Baker, Mike Stone, who had engineered many of Queen's greatest albums, including co-producing *News Of The World* with them.

With Cain, Journey brought a new sound into the studio. A few critics found fault with it, like music critic Gary Graff, who said, 'Each song sounds less distinctive and more like the work of another band.' Deborah Frost, in *Rolling Stone*, who had a few kind words for 'Who's Cryin' Now', was still brutally snarky, giving it a 'passing grade' in 'Advanced Jukebox Muzak'. She absolutely hated the rest of the album, calling it 'a triumph of professionalism, a veritable march of the well-versed schmaltz stirrers.'

Other critics praised its pop hooks and predicted it would make a lot of money. Commercial success is evidence of a lack of serious artistic vision for critics like Frost. The fans made it Journey's top-selling studio album ever. *Escape* is their only *Billboard* Hot 200 album to hit number one. It also charted in many other countries, which made it by far their biggest worldwide success. The album produced four hit singles on the Hot 100 and a fifth song, 'Stone In Love', climbed the mainstream rock charts. The album reached diamond status in the United States with over ten million copies sold. The *Escape* tour started in June 1981, and after a January to March winter break, it picked back up in April and continued to July 1982. The singles and the touring kept this on the charts for 154 weeks.

Escape pushed Journey to such heights that it led to a silly marketing ploy. They created a video game, *Journey Escape*, for the Atari 2600 console, released in 1982. Players guide each band member to the scarab spaceship and must avoid losing money to groupies, photographers, concert promoters, and crowd barriers. Herbie even shows up to give them a cash boost on occasion. It is a mind-numbingly terrible 8-bit experience. You can find videos of gameplay for this. Unfortunately, it would not be the last time they dabbled in video games. In 1983, they licensed a second game, this time hiring Bally/Midway to create an arcade game. Arcades, brick-and-mortar spaces filled with pinball machines and video games, were very popular in the early 1980s. This game featured digitized headshots of the band members, and the player had to help each of them retrieve their instruments and dodge bad guys. It's as tedious as it sounds. Fortunately, this was the final time they ventured into this space.

Escape also forced some technical innovation from Herbie. Nightmare, Journey's parent company, kept as much of the touring expenditures as possible in-house. Travel, recording, lighting, sound, and more were all owned and run by Nocturne, a subsidiary of Nightmare. Because Journey was moving out of arenas and into stadiums, Herbie proposed using innovative (at the time) video technology to create gigantic screens on each side of the stage so that people sitting far away could see the performers up close during the show. This innovation became the norm for large shows. Nocturne made even more money renting out these services to other musical acts when Journey were not on the road.

Escape's cover, once again by Stanley Mouse, shows the scarab bursting out of a planet, shattering its surface. The title is spelled with a mix of numbers and letters: E5C4P3. The rear cover art is the scarab accelerating toward the familiar Journey planet with its torus ring. The sleeve features the band in black fills, like a reverse negative.

'Don't Stop Believin'' (Perry, Schon, Cain) 4:09

The Hammond B3 of Gregg Rolie has been replaced by the Yamaha C7 of Jonathan Cain, and it makes its appearance at the very beginning on side one, cut one of *Escape*. The iconic bass and piano opening, heard on radio stations and karaoke bars across the world, leads to the lyrics, 'Just a small-town girl, livin' in a lonely world, she took the midnight train going anywhere'. Now, this is different because it sounds more like a story setup than a love song. Next comes the notorious line, 'Just a city boy, born and raised in south Detroit, he took the midnight train going anywhere'. By now, the world knows that 'south' Detroit does not exist. If you head south across the Detroit River, then you will find yourself in Canada, specifically Windsor, Ontario. Yet, the mistake sounds great and adds to the charm of the song.

As we approach the one-minute mark, a simple guitar melody rises from the bass line. Schon increases volume and speed as he emulates a train coming to a screeching halt. The girl and boy are in a new world: 'A singer in a smoky room, the smell of wine and cheap perfume, for a smile they can share the night, it goes on and on and on'. These words come from the memories of both Cain and Perry and their days working in the California club circuit, evoking the nighttime situation of so many lost and lonely people.

Smith's drums enter to set up a faux chorus: 'Strangers waiting, up and down the boulevard. They're shadows searching in the night. Streetlights, people, livin' just to find emotion. Hiding somewhere in the night'. Looking down from his Detroit hotel room in the darkness inspired Perry to write the lyrics about streetlights and people.

After a short melodic bridge, without a guitar solo (!), the next verse begins in the first person: 'Working hard to get my fill. Everybody wants a thrill, payin' anything to roll the dice just one more time'. Then, sticking with the metaphor for taking chances: 'Some will win, some will lose, some are going to sing the blues. Oh, the movie never ends, it goes on and on and on and on'.

This leads to a repeat of the faux chorus. On its dramatic peak, Schon fires up the guitar and plays the melody of the real chorus. It's a spectacular moment in pop music. Perry and the band sing the chorus – 'Don't stop believin', hold onto to that feelin'. Streetlight, people' –which repeats to a fadeout. The song's title comes from Jonathan Cain's notebooks. When Cain was thinking the music business might not work out for him, he called home to Chicago and talked to his father, who told Cain not to give up and said, 'Son, don't stop believing.' He found the words in his notebook when they were writing songs for *Escape*.

The song was their second single from the album (with the B-side 'Natural Thing'), released in the fall of 1981, peaking at number nine in December. It stayed on the charts for 16 weeks. It also spent 28 weeks on the *Mainstream Rock Airplay* chart, peaking at number eight. 'Who's Cryin' Now' and 'Open Arms' were bigger hits at the time. However, 'Don't Stop Believin'' has become their most popular song. It has been used at sporting events, in movies and on television and was in the jukebox musical *Rock Of Ages*, each appearance spurring renewed interest. It sold over seven million digital downloads, considered the most for a song recorded before 2000.

The song was used in the final moments of the series finale of the popular television show *The Sopranos* (2007) and in the pilot episode of *Glee* in 2009. It also had a major resurgence on the UK charts in the 2010s thanks to its use in competition shows like *The X Factor*. 'Don't Stop Believin'' is collected on *Greatest Hits* and *Time³* and was included on the original soundtrack for the movie *Monster* in 2003.

'Stone In Love' (Perry, Schon, Cain) 4:24
A simple guitar phrase kicks off this straightforward rocker. Rock bands often write wistful lyrics about the fun they used to have in their younger days and 'Stone In Love' is a classic of the genre. Schon's original title was 'Stoned In Love', but Perry and Cain reworked it into this form. With limited opportunities for keyboards here, Cain is pressed into duty on rhythm guitar. It is a solid power pop track with a touch of wistful nostalgia that has kept it on the live set lists over the years.

The song hit the *Billboard* Mainstream Rock Airplay charts in the US, peaking at 13 in August 1981 and staying on the charts for 20 weeks. It was released in the UK and the Netherlands in 1982 with the B-side 'Only Solutions'. It's collected on *Greatest Hits 2* and *Time³*.

'Who's Cryin' Now' (Perry, Cain) 4:59
Another opening with bass and piano, this minor key intro feels like melancholy is heading our way. This was a curious choice for the first single from the album, but in contrast to 'Don't Stop Believin'', it does have a regular verse-chorus structure. Despite the downer lyrics about heartbreak, tears and unfulfilled desire, it has a catchy melody and is easy to sing. Two things stand out for me on this track: first, during the bridge, Perry sings, 'Only so many tears you can cry, 'til the heartache is over, and now you can say, your love ... will never die'. When he sings 'your love', he delivers a slight vocal fry with an emotional rawness that I have not heard any later Journey lead singer attempt. The second standout moment is the guitar solo that takes the song to its fadeout. It's a fabulous 80 seconds of music, reminiscent of George Benson or Pat Metheny in its simplicity and musicianship.

'Who's Cryin' Now' (with the B-side 'Mother, Father') was Journey's first top ten single in the US. Released in July 1981, it peaked at number four on the *Billboard* Hot 100 in October. It stayed on the chart for 21 weeks. It reached number four and spent 20 weeks on the Mainstream Rock Airplay chart. It spent 17 weeks on the Adult Contemporary chart, hitting as high as number 14. The song is collected on *Greatest Hits* and *Time³*.

'Keep On Runnin'' (Perry, Schon, Cain) 3:38

The first song that Cain, Perry and Schon co-wrote together is a fast, guitar-driven rocker. The album has a couple of these on each side of the vinyl, and these melodic rock tunes, for better or worse, became blueprints for many songs to come throughout the 1980s and early 1990s. Pop metal (or hair metal) adopted these approaches. Schon's guitar is heard throughout the song with no letup. This is Cain's take on the 'blue collar' world of Journey's audience. It makes its point about working hard for little money and no prospects of advancement, where making it to the weekend is the most important goal. The song was a concert staple throughout the 1980s. This track is collected on *Time³*.

'Still They Ride' (Perry, Schon, Cain) 3:49

Side one ends with this slow ballad. Valory provides a thick bass line, with piano and guitar adding flourishes to Perry's on-point vocals. The lyrics are about a man, Jesse, driving the streets of the town of his youth. The town's changed, but others now cruise the streets as he did. There's a sentimentality in Perry's voice as he sings about the challenge of moving on from such a place: 'It's hard to leave this carousel'. According to the *Time³* liner notes, this type of nostalgic California scene of kids cruising also inspired George Lucas, back in 1973, to create *American Graffiti*.

'Still They Ride' was the fourth single (with the B-side 'La Raza Del Sol'). It was released in May 1982 and peaked at number 19, two weeks before the one-year anniversary of the album's release. It spent time on the Adult Contemporary chart, peaking at 37 for four weeks and the Mainstream Rock Airplay chart, peaking at 47 for two weeks. The track is collected on *Greatest Hits 2* and *Time³*.

'Escape' (Perry, Schon, Cain) 5:16

The title song opens side two of the vinyl release, and it served as the concert opener for the *Escape* tour. It is a musical hodgepodge featuring multiple distinct themes. Cain has been acknowledged for cataloging the various riffs and melodies Schon captured over the years on the guitarist's home four-track recorder. Cain arranged some of these stray elements to create 'Escape'. Despite Smith's contributions to the arrangements during recording, it didn't result in a songwriting credit for him.

Schon plays a riff before everyone joins in the shuffle. This first part's chorus – 'They won't take me. They won't break me' – is supplemented by Cain's rhythmic piano playing. There is a guitar and keyboard buildup that leads into a new section at the 2:02 mark. Schon's guitar takes up what will become the vocal melody for a couple of bars before Perry sings a call-and-response with the band, 'I'm finally out. I'm clear and I'm free'; the backing vocals respond, 'I've got dreams I'm living for'.

Next comes a new version of the chorus, leading with the line, 'I'll break away. Yes, I'm on my way. Oh, I will leave there today. Yes, I'm on my way'. Perry then repeats the chorus in full, and with that, we reach the guitar solo at the 3:48 mark.

The song concludes by reprising the chorus, this time with backing vocals and then a short restatement of the punchy rhythm from earlier before fading on a sustained note from Cain's synthesizer. To me, this is a terrific Frankenstein's monster of a song. I especially like the vocal arrangements. 'Escape' is collected on *Greatest Hits 2*.

'Lay It Down' (Perry, Schon, Cain) 4:12
'Lay It Down' would fit comfortably on any album by Poison, Ratt, or Mötley Crüe. This brand of pop metal didn't take off in the United States for another couple of years, but when it did, it sounded a lot like 'Lay It Down'. The song isn't bad, but it isn't all that good in comparison to the rest of this album.

Perry isn't a screamer or a growler, and songs like this, to me, sound better with these types of vocals. Perry has the range to sing those high notes without the need for a falsetto. Compare him to a singer with a similar range, for example, Steelheart's Miljenko Matijevic – there is a clear difference in how the high notes are handled, with Perry's performance sounding too polished, too clean.

As a straightforward rocker, 'Lay It Down' checks the box, though it never really found a spot in live performances.

'Dead Or Alive' (Perry, Schon, Cain) 3:20
By far the fastest song on *Escape*, 'Dead Or Alive' is a hard rock tune with a driving boogie shuffle. A relentless workout for Smith and Valory, with Cain pounding away on the piano, Schon takes center stage throughout the track. The song is about a hit man, exemplified by the chorus: 'Wanted dead or alive. Blood for money, money. Assault, homicide. Blood for money, money'. They even mention a Maserati. The band's unrestrained attack gets the blood pumping. Perry's vocals take a back seat here. If I read too deeply into the song, it could be about Schon and his inability to NOT play the guitar, as we will see during the winter break of the *Escape* tour. In the meantime, you could play this track during your intense gym workouts.

'Mother, Father' (Schon, Perry, Cain, M. Schon) 5:28
A gorgeous piano melody accompanied by acoustic guitar opens this song by the band's primary composition trio, along with Neal's father, Matthew. 'Mother, Father' is about a son trying to heal his parents' broken marriage. The lyrics describe the effects of the conflict on each of them and the pleas not to give up, given what they have built and felt until now. There's a

maturity to the song that directly conflicts with the notion that Journey turned shallow when they went 'commercial', a word that, around this time, Perry challenged critics to define. He suggested it meant that they sold more albums: 'What are we supposed to do?' he asked. My point is that perhaps the band's songwriting maturation had a lot to do with their success. Did they go too far with radio-friendly ballads? We will discuss this on subsequent albums.

While not as musically diverse as 'Escape', this track has fine transitions and some excellent playing by every band member. Smith and Valory continue their roles as *Escape*'s unsung heroes. Their work on this track is stellar. Schon plays some exquisite guitar during the first bridge, with its interesting chord progression courtesy of his father. 'Mother, Father' is in the key of G, with Neal's solo starting around the 2:04 mark with an E minor chord, and during the first pass, there is an interesting tonal shift (2:11) before a return to E minor (2:19). On the second pass, this progression is repeated, but an additional chord is added that leaves the solo feeling unresolved (2:34), which matches the unresolved conflict in the lyrics.

Perry delivers the final dramatic verse: 'Through bitter tears and wounded years, those ties of blood were strong. So much to say, those yesterdays, so now don't you turn away'. He brings the desperate need, willing these unhappy people not to give up. As the chorus says at its end, 'Have faith, believe'. At the 3:54 mark, Schon turns in one of his seminal solos. The many live versions of this song are all worth a listen, even if only for these moments.

The band return for the final chorus, and with the final 30 seconds, Smith transitions them into a fitting denouement. Perry sings 'Have faith' and 'Believe' in a quiet, supplicating way, Smith loading the gaps with drum fills. The concluding section is a triumphal piano and guitar melody, with Perry delivering a signature haunting, angelic vocalese before a quiet guitar fade.

While this is not a sing-along pop hit, it deserves more attention and appreciation. The track was the B-side to the single 'Who's Cryin' Now' and is collected on *Time*[3].

'Open Arms' (Perry, Cain) 3:19

When originally brought to rehearsals, Schon asked, 'What are we supposed to play on that song?' He had a point. Even John Waite skipped the opportunity to record this with The Babys. For those who were already critical of the band, it served as proof that Journey were doing this for the money. As Steve Perry said, 'Of course we are.' And other bands had scored their biggest hits with ballads. Styx reached number one with 'Babe' in 1979. In the fall of 1981, Foreigner scored a massive number-two hit with 'Waiting For A Girl Like You'. An arena rock band recording a ballad was not only not unprecedented but also a key ingredient in financial success.

The question for bands that have success with a ballad is, are you going to write another one? For Journey, specifically Jonathan Cain, the answer would

The band backstage in Oklahoma City, Oklahoma, on 8 April 1980 during the *Departure* tour. Gregg Rolie is dressed for the home crowd. (*Alamy*)

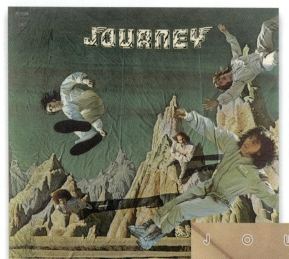

Left: The original five members on 1975's *Journey*: Neal Schon and George Tickner (standing), and Aynsley Dunbar, Gregg Rolie and Ross Valory (floating). (*Columbia*)

Right: The self-produced *Look Into The Future* has Journey's only studio cover: George Harrison's Beatles song 'It's All Too Much'. (*Columbia*)

Left: *Next* was the last album without a dedicated lead vocalist. Rolie was joined by Schon on the mic here. (*Columbia*)

Right: Alton Kelley and Stanley Mouse deliver their wing motif on *Infinity*, the first album with Steve Perry and the final for Aynsley Dunbar. (*Columbia*)

Left: *Evolution* was the final cover that featured Kelley and Mouse working together. It's also the first album with Steve Smith. (*Columbia*)

Right: Alton Kelley worked alone on *Departure*'s cover. This was the last album with Gregg Rolie. (*Columbia*)

Above: The quartet – Schon, Dunbar, Valory and Rolie – from the back cover of the 1977 album *Next*.

Below: Journey opened for Santana for four dates in the Netherlands in late 1976, billed as the 'Amigos' in 'Europa' tour. (*Barry Schultz*)

Right: Neal Schon live onstage, without his horseshoe moustache, circa 1981.

Below: The *Infinity* lineup, 1979: Schon, Aynsley Dunbar, Rolie, Valory and the new vocalist, Steve Perry. (*Alamy*)

Above: Robert Fleischman, Journey's first pure lead vocalist, was dismissed in favor of Steve Perry before the recording of *Infinity*. (*Getty*)

Below: The band performing on the *Infinity* tour in 1978. (*Getty*)

With their rising success, they're all smiles in this publicity photo for the *Evolution* tour in June 1979. (*Michael Putland/Getty Images*)

Below: Perry and Schon on stage in New York in 1980. (*Richard E Aaron/Redferns*)

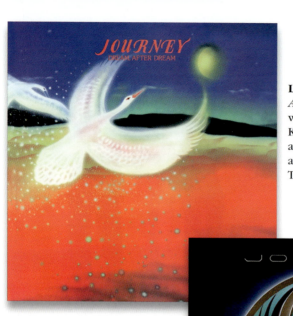

Left: The cover for the *Dream, After Dream* soundtrack album was illustrated by Koichi Kubodera and was based on a concept from Aki Morishita and the film's director Kenzo Takada. (*Columbia*)

Right: *Captured* was the second cover designed by a solo Stanley Mouse. (*Columbia*)

Left: Stanley Mouse created the *Escape* cover, the band's most commercially successful album and the first to feature Jonathan Cain. (*Columbia*)

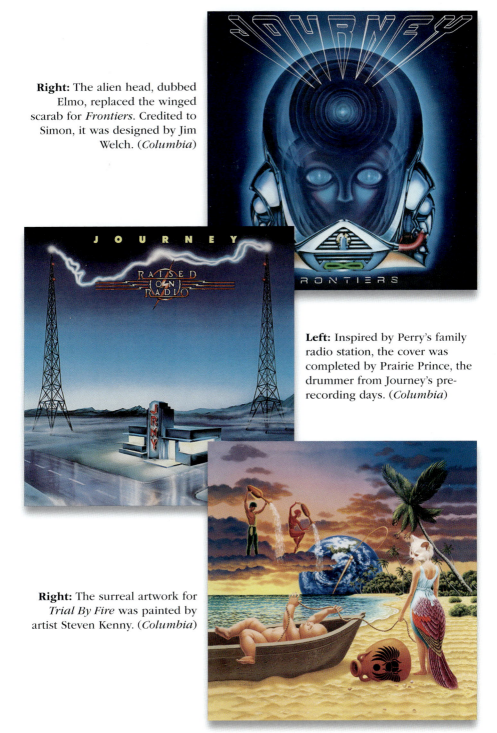

Right: The alien head, dubbed Elmo, replaced the winged scarab for *Frontiers*. Credited to Simon, it was designed by Jim Welch. (*Columbia*)

Left: Inspired by Perry's family radio station, the cover was completed by Prairie Prince, the drummer from Journey's pre-recording days. (*Columbia*)

Right: The surreal artwork for *Trial By Fire* was painted by artist Steven Kenny. (*Columbia*)

Above: Journey's classic lineup circa 1981: Cain, Valory, Schon, Perry, Smith. (*Roger Ressmeyer/Corbis*)

Left: Perry performing 'Separate Ways (Worlds Apart)' on a cool New Orleans morning for the infamous music video. (*Getty*)

Above: The *Raised On Radio* lineup, 1986: Perry, Randy Jackson, Cain, Mike Baird, Schon.

Below: Cain, Randy Jackson and Schon on the opening night of the *Raised On Radio* tour, Angels Camp, California, 23 August 1986. (*Larry Hulst/Michael Ochs Archives/Getty*)

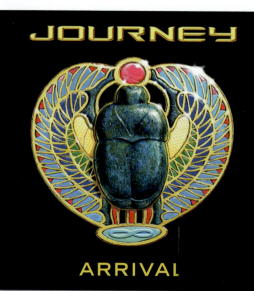

Left: The first album with Steve Augeri, *Arrival* was Journey's final album for Columbia Records. (*Columbia*)

Right: This simple, original *Red 13* cover got an update on the Frontiers Records release with a design by fan Christopher Payne. (*Journey*)

Left: Recorded at The Record Plant, where they made *Raised On Radio*, *Generations* was the last album with Augeri. (*Sanctuary*)

Right: Released exclusively via Wal-Mart stores, *Revelation* featured new music and a re-recording of 11 of the greatest hits with new singer Arnel Pineda. (*Nomota*)

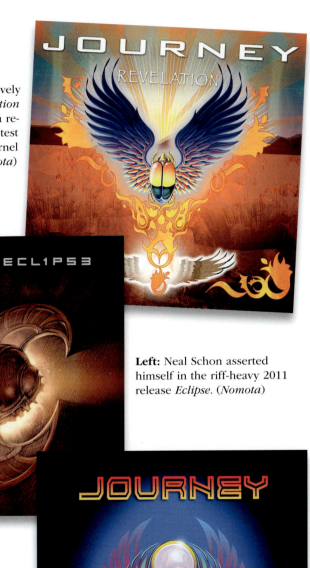

Left: Neal Schon asserted himself in the riff-heavy 2011 release *Eclipse*. (*Nomota*)

Right: The 2022 studio album *Freedom* featured the drumming and composing contributions of producer Narada Michael Walden. (*BMG*)

Above: Steve Augeri took on the difficult task of replacing Steve Perry as Journey's frontman. (*Tim Mosenfelder/ImageDirect/Getty*)

Below: New singer Arnel Pineda with Schon and Castronovo in Manila on 2 March 2009. They recorded *Live In Manila* on 14 March. (*AP Photo/Aaron Favila, File*)

Above: Neal Schon's Journey Through Time in San Francisco on 9 February 2018: Castronovo, Schon, Marco Mendoza (bass), Rolie, John Varn (keyboards). (*Tim Mosenfelder, Getty*)

Below: Schon and Pineda in Nashville, Tennessee, on 27 April 2022. Jason Derlatka provides additional keyboards and vocals. (*Getty*)

Left: An advertisement for *Captured*, Journey's first live album.

Below: An ad for the *Journey Escape* video game, released for the Atari 2600 in 1982. A different arcade game from Bally followed the next year.

be 'yes' and, in my opinion, it colors Journey's output from this point on. We'll touch on these attempts at balladry as we look at each track throughout the rest of the book. For now, we should view this as a watershed moment in Journey's history for good or ill.

Cain's piano melody is instantly recognizable. In concert, he often plays it directly after his keyboard solo, which allows for an easy transition from solo to song and gives the audience a reason to cheer louder. Perry sings with proper tenderness and angst: 'Lying beside you, here in the dark, feeling your heartbeat with mine'. Cain wrote the lyrics for his then-wife, Tané, and performed it at their wedding. While it is easy to view as syrupy sweet, the deft writing conveys a clear message about a man who has only had this one love in his life and realizes this after a period of separation. The powerful chorus – 'So here I am, with open arms, hoping you'll see what your love means to me. Open arms' – delivers a strong, forceful sentiment when sung by Perry. It is a potent love song and, like *Frontiers*' 'Faithfully', has been a popular wedding tune.

From an instrumental standpoint, this is a piano song. The guitar chords and rhythm section serve as little more than a support for the vocals. A short bridge, beginning at 1:30, has Cain playing softly like he's on a Lionel Richie ballad. Schon bends a few notes, but you will not find any soulful solos here. (The string orchestra accompaniment on Journey ballads will have to wait for *Trial By Fire*.) As part of Journey's core hits, the song is performed at every Journey concert.

Barely three minutes long, the song took off upon its release in January 1982. Journey's biggest commercial hit, it peaked at number two by late February and stayed on the *Billboard* Hot 100 for 18 weeks. It spent 19 weeks on the Adult Contemporary chart, peaking at number seven. For the Mainstream Rock Airplay chart, it peaked at 35 and lasted for ten weeks.

'Open Arms' was the third single from *Escape* and had 'Little Girl' from *Dream, After Dream* as its B-side. It was also included on the original soundtrack for the movie *Heavy Metal* in 1981 (the movie was an anthology of short, animated films connected loosely in an overarching story). 'Open Arms' was featured in the 'Harry Canyon' segment. The track is collected on *Greatest Hits* and *Time*[3].

Related Tracks
'La Raza Del Sol' (Perry, Cain) 3:26
A literal translation is 'The Sun Race', but a better take is 'The Sun People', which refers to the migrant laborers in California's agricultural sector. Cain, inspired by a book about these workers, wrote the song about people's desire to make a life in another country. The lyrics keep the perspective on the man who will 'follow the sun to the great river valley' and 'find a life 'cross the border'.

Valory's bassline provides a sense of Latin-style rhythm. Smith plays a shuffle, but there are no congas to be found here. Schon stays in a rhythm guitar supporting role until the 2:15 mark when he begins his solo. To me, this solo sounds like a throwback to his Santana days. Compare it with his work on 'Song Of The Wind' on *Caravanserai*.

The song was the odd one out for *Escape*, though it was used as the B-side for 'Still They Ride'. 'La Raza Del Sol' was added as a bonus track on the 2006 CD release of *Escape* and is collected on *Time³*. Journey perform a tremendous live version of this as an encore on their *Live In Japan 2017* album.

'Only Solutions' (Cain, Schon, Perry) 3:33
Journey were at their commercial apex as 1982 dawned. They were on a break from touring for the winter months but were offered a chance to contribute a couple of songs for the new high-tech Disney movie *Tron*, which was about a computer hacker who is digitized and forced to compete in various games in cyberspace. Wendy Carlos, of *Switched-On Bach* fame, had already written and recorded the soundtrack. Journey's two tracks were added afterwards.

Cain and Schon wrote the music with a poppy guitar melody intro and a routine solo during the bridge. Perry changed the lyrics to his satisfaction. He delivers the verses with a staccato rhythm, heavily stressing the end of each line – 'Faces, numbers, I recognize. You don't fool me with cynical lies' and so on. The drone of the chorus isn't offensive, but it doesn't help the listenability. It was recorded with a drum loop, which, per the *Time³* liner notes, Smith then overdubbed. Schon remarked that it sounded hastily thrown together because it was indeed hastily thrown together.

'Only Solutions' spent five weeks on the *Mainstream Rock Airplay* chart, peaking at a modest number 22. Added as a B-side to 'Stone In Love' in countries where that song was released as a single, it is also on the *Tron Soundtrack* (1982) and collected on *Time³*.

'1990's Theme' (Schon, Cain) 2:25
If 'Only Solutions' sounds 'thrown together', then this instrumental track sounds like a demo for a Casio keyboard and The Jaminator, which was a toy guitar synthesizer on the market in the early 1990s. I had one, and it sounded identical to Schon's work on this track. This is all meant to evoke computers as only 1980s music can do. It isn't terrible; it's just slight. There are the makings of a solid instrumental here, but that isn't the purpose this serves, so we only have this fragment of what could have been. The only place to find this tune is on the *Tron Soundtrack*, which is out of print, though you can find recordings online.

The 2006 CD release of *Escape* has three other bonus tracks in addition to 'La Raza Del Sol': 'Don't Stop Believin", 'Who's Cryin' Now' and 'Open Arms', which are all from *Live In Houston, 11/6/1981,* which was released in 2005 on CD and DVD and is covered separately.

Frontiers (1983)

Personnel:
Jonathan Cain: keyboards, guitar, vocals
Steve Perry: lead vocals
Neal Schon: guitar, vocals
Steve Smith: drums
Ross Valory: bass, vocals
Produced by Mike Stone and Kevin Elson
Engineered by Mike Stone
Recorded and mixed at Fantasy Studios, Berkeley, California
Assistant Engineer: Wally Buck
US release date: 1 February 1983
Highest chart position: US: 2; 6x Platinum Certified
Running time: 44:09

The seeds of discontent were sown during the height of Journey's success. Neal Schon always seemed to be involved in some musical project and always needed to be working, creating and playing guitar. He is that way to this day. During the lull between the end of the *Departure* tour and the making of *Dream, After Dream* (which only took a week) and the beginning of the *Escape* studio sessions, Schon went out on his own for a bit. He teamed up with jazz and rock keyboardist and drummer Jan Hammer and the left-handed jazz and blues bassist Colin Hodgkinson to record *Untold Passion* under the name Schon & Hammer, which was released in November 1981. Schon did the lead vocals in addition to the guitar. This was a watershed event in the Journey annals. Sure, Schon had done occasional session work on a track here or there during Journey's limited downtime, but he was the first active member to record an entire record as a different musical act. Schon could safely say this was not a threat. He was flexing his musical muscles, performing music that Journey would likely never do. Herbie managed Schon & Hammer and long-time designer and art director Jim Welch, who worked on most of Journey's albums, also worked on *Untold Passions*. Kelley even did the cover art. For good or ill, though, he set the precedent for doing independent solo work.

Refusing to let the downtime after the *Escape* tour go to waste, Schon & Hammer (and Hodgkinson) reunited for 1982's *Here To Stay*. This contained the minor MTV hit 'No More Lies'. One track on the album featured every member of Journey for a song co-written by Schon, Cain and Perry called 'Self Defense', which Schon sings while Perry supplies backing vocals. This de facto Journey tune would be recorded in 2005 for inclusion on *Generations*, with Schon still behind the mic, under the title 'In Self Defense'.

Not that everyone else was lounging on the beach during the break in 1982. Steve Perry co-wrote and shared lead vocals on one of the best pop-rock hits of the early 1980s. The lead track on Kenny Loggins's *High Adventure* called

'Don't Fight It' featured Pat Benatar's husband Neil 'Spyder' Giraldo on guitar. This number 17 hit in the late summer of 1982 whetted Perry's appetite for working on his own music. Furthermore, Jonathan Cain wrote, played on, sang backing vocals on and co-produced his wife's first and only album, *Tané Cain*. Schon even lent some guitar work to the record.

A bigger surprise than a Tané Cain solo album came from Steve Smith. Ready to scratch the jazz itch he had since working with Jean-Luc Ponty, he formed an ensemble, Vital Information, and released an all-instrumental eponymous debut in January 1983. This raised Smith's profile in the professional drumming world, showing off his creativity and versatility.

Meanwhile, the band had to create a follow-up to *Escape*. As Cain described it, they had to act as if they were not riding high on a successful album. They needed to stay hungry and humble and keep writing songs. Any band would love to achieve this level of success, but the pressure to meet or exceed expectations can lead to making a copycat album, which comes with the accusations of formulaic songwriting. Then there's the risk of going in the opposite direction, taking experimentation a bit too far and alienating fans. Or adopting the most difficult path of moderation, finding that middle ground of the familiar but new, taking a few calculated risks and getting back on the road. As we will see, they might have taken all three of these approaches on this record.

There are a few other events that sowed those seeds of discontent besides the solo projects. For the first time, Herbie did not prevent interference from Columbia about song selection. Michael Dilbeck, the A&R representative, had pulled what would become two staples of Journey's repertoire from the album – 'Ask The Lonely' and 'Only The Young' – and replaced them with 'Troubled Child' and 'Back Talk'. To this point, thanks to shrewd contracts from Herbie, the band always had the final say on what was included on their records.

The band were also making serious money. Nightmare Productions, which controlled the recording and merchandising side of the business, and Nocturne Productions, which handled the concerts, including transportation, lighting, stages, sound and those huge video screens, were a well-oiled, well-operated machine with little debt and made all involved very wealthy. When making this sort of money, the arduous work of touring might lose some of its urgency. And life on the road was taking its toll on relationships, too. Ross Valory and Neal Schon were both going through divorces, which, as we will see, led to the first track on *Frontiers*.

The album was released at the beginning of February 1983, hit the *Billboard* 200 about two weeks later and peaked at number two in March. It stayed on the charts for 85 weeks and spawned four hit singles. By all standards, it was a successful follow-up but not an improvement over *Escape*. Journey had reached its commercial peak. They would start their tour with a couple of weeks in Japan on 22 February 1983. They would then come back to the United States, culminating with five nights in Honolulu before ending the tour on 6 September.

For the first time since *Next*, the final artwork did not come from Kelley or Mouse. Jim Welch used an illustration credited to Simon. It was an alien with a huge cranium inside a transparent helmet with built-in headphones, known throughout Journey fandom as 'Elmo'. No scarab and no feathers were to be found on this one. Mouse had created a cover, which featured an alien, though seated and holding a large pink orb. It did not look very Journey-like either and, according to Herbie, Steve Perry balked at the imagery. If this story is true, it is important as a reflection of the growing struggle for control between Herbie Herbert and Steve Perry.

'Separate Ways (Worlds Apart)' (Perry, Cain) 5:23
Perry and Cain wrote this for the band members going through breakups. This is their first synthesizer-focused rock song, which was a sign of the times in 1983. Schon's guitar embellishments and his crunchy chords add heft and interest to a solid melodic rocker. Add the weight of Smith's drums to this satisfying rhythm, and this fan favorite became a staple of classic rock radio. Written during the *Escape* tour, the band debuted the song before recording it, and audiences responded enthusiastically, ensuring its inclusion on *Frontiers*.

We must address the music video. Universally scorned and mercilessly criticized, especially in the animated show *Beavis And Butt-Head*, the video features the entire band lip-syncing and playing air instruments on a dock while a young woman walks by in a leather skirt. Closeups show various band members singing into the side of her face. There is no story here; nothing imaginative is happening. The video looks like something a few school kids pieced together at the last minute to avoid receiving a failing grade in film school. The video is on the *Greatest Hits DVD 1978-1997* and is a must-watch, though be prepared to cringe. The band agreed after this and other *Frontiers* videos that future video releases would be pure performance films, either in the studio or on stage.

'Separate Ways (Worlds Apart)' was the first single (with the B-side 'Frontiers') from *Frontiers*, hitting the charts on 1 February 1983 and peaking at number eight in March. It stayed on the *Billboard* chart for 17 weeks. The song also hit number one for four weeks on the *Billboard* Mainstream Rock Airplay chart, where it lingered for 25 weeks. It is on *Time³* and *Greatest Hits*.

'Send Her My Love' (Perry, Cain) 3:54
Cain hears words and phrases, and his brain begins to turn them into a song. This is the case with 'Send Her My Love', which was triggered by an exchange with a fan from Cain's native Chicago. The person said that his former girlfriend said to say 'Hello', and Cain replied, 'Send her my love', then his next thought, according to his memoirs, was, 'That's a song.'

It begins like a maudlin ballad, opening with a quiet keyboard note and a steady rim click from Smith. Schon does a little more with the guitar parts here than he did on 'Open Arms', playing full melodic parts instead of a sprinkling of notes. Perry brings a heavy, soulful melancholy to his vocals. The choruses build in intensity, from well-placed accents at the end of verses to an efficient, if unremarkable, guitar solo.

Perry calls this one of his favorites, and it is an enjoyable four-minute listen. It deserved its release as the fourth single (with the B-side 'Back Talk') in September 1983. It reached number 23 on the Billboard Hot 100 in November and stayed on the charts for 15 weeks while also charting as high as number 27 on the Adult Contemporary chart, where it lasted ten weeks. The song is on *Time^3* and *Greatest Hits*.

'Chain Reaction' (Perry, Schon, Cain) 4:19

One of their signature pop-metal tracks, 'Chain Reaction' is guitar-driven, with call-and-response verses and a simple chorus. The song thunders along from beginning to end, with a chorus intended for fan participation – it's always a crowd-pleaser in the arena. While not included on the *Greatest Hits DVD 1978-1997*, you should check out the non-concert video for this track. A little better than 'Separate Ways', here the boys wear tuxedos and perform on a set that looks like a modern bar collided with a 1950s ice cream parlor. The video will still induce a cringe or two. Expect fresh hairstyles, some dance moves, a bit of acting and a repeated image of Schon making moves on a mannequin (yikes); during his final solo, Schon demonstrates the flexibility of his quadriceps. It's not a great video, but it is a fun piece of the 1980s and Journey's history. 'Chain Reaction' is on *Greatest Hits 2*.

'After The Fall' (Perry, Cain) 5:00

For those deep into band lore, 'After The Fall' is a key plot point in the story of the lineup shakeup prior to the recording of *Raised On Radio*. Per *Time^3*'s liner notes, Perry wrote the chorus while playing around on bass. There are lyrical passages that are vintage Cain, but the music is mostly written by Perry, with uncredited help from Smith. The bass groove proved difficult for Valory to get exactly right, so to keep things moving in the studio, Smith recommended a bassist he had worked with before named Randy Jackson. The band loved him. He plays bass, uncredited, on this track, though he does get a 'Special Thanks' in the *Frontiers* liner notes. Was this a crack in the band's armor? One guest appearance isn't the cause of a breakup, but it is part of the story.

'After The Fall' is one of the three tracks subjected to Journey's notorious non-concert video treatment. The set for this one is a darkened room that features different band members and furniture configurations throughout the song. The video is mainly Perry lip-syncing, but various band members get their moments faking it on their instruments, including Valory slapping away on a Steinberger on a song he didn't record. There are also silly moments of each of them falling through the air outside the window. Like 'Chain Reaction', the video isn't particularly terrible, but it is not very imaginative. The band appear to be going through the motions for the record label's MTV needs.

Unfortunately, 'After The Fall' isn't routinely played in concert. Released as the third single (with the B-side 'Rubicon') in July 1983, it peaked at number 23 in August 1983 and spent 12 weeks on the *Billboard* Hot 100 chart. The song made a tiny bit of noise on the Mainstream Rock Airplay chart, hitting number 30, but only lasted four weeks. The song is on the soundtrack for the movie *Risky Business* and is collected on *Greatest Hits 2* and *Time*[3].

'Faithfully' (Cain) 4:27

Depending on your musical preference, the first side of *Frontiers* ends with transcendence or disappointment. Most fans go with the positive view, as 'Faithfully' is one of the iconic ballads of 1980s American pop music. Cain has told the story many times of how the song came to him while on tour. He wanted to capture the monotony of being alone on the road. The song, in my opinion, improves upon the blueprint set by 'Open Arms', this time with better lyrics and Perry wringing an even greater amount of emotion from the verses and the chorus. Schon's guitar parts make for a powerful finish to the track.

The accompanying video mixes concert film with scenes from the tour bus and the dressing rooms. The video gives some interesting, staged moments, such as Cain staring in a mirror with Tané's photo tucked in the lower corner, which became ironic given she is the intended recipient of the song and her alleged infidelities at the time. There are also 'live' non-concert clips, such as the adorable footage of Steve Smith bringing his baby up the stairs to the jet. These candid shots document the life on the road in a more sincere and authentic manner than the staged ones from Cain and the weird image of Perry preparing to remove his shaving cream-covered mustache.

'Faithfully' deserves its accolades. It was the second single released in April 1983 (with the B-side 'Edge Of The Blade'), peaking at number 12 on the *Billboard* charts and staying on the charts for 16 weeks. The song is on *Greatest Hits* and *Time*[3].

'Edge Of The Blade' (Perry, Schon, Cain) 4:30

We begin the second side of *Frontiers*. No hits come from side two, but some of the more interesting tracks from Journey happen when they are cutting loose or experimenting and not aiming for the charts. 'Edge Of The Blade' sits in the 'cutting loose' category. An energetic workout built around a classic Schon riff, the song would fit on most pop metal or hard rock albums of the decade or even as a track on Journey's 2011 album *Eclipse*. The guitar dominates, with strong support from the rhythm section and color from

Cain's piano. Perry's vocals are strong, but he doesn't sound comfortable on this type of hard rock tune. 'Edge Of The Blade' was the B-side to 'Faithfully' and was a staple on the *Frontiers* tour.

'Troubled Child' (Perry, Schon, Cain) 4:29
Here is our second minor key track for side two. This song about a young person on the streets doesn't say much. The lyrics are mostly phrases strung together describing the person of the title, like an artist making a quick sketch portrait. The vocals are muddy, but that is probably on purpose to keep the song from sounding incongruously bright. Perry holds the word 'moon' for ten seconds before the chorus begins. The melody isn't memorable as 'Troubled Child' lacks a strong hook. It is rarely played live.

This song and the next also have the dubious distinction of being the tracks that replaced two beloved classics: 'Ask The Lonely' and 'Only The Young'. Interestingly, 'Troubled Child' was the B-side of 'Ask The Lonely' when released as a single in Japan.

'Back Talk' (Perry, Cain, Smith) 3:16
When Steve Smith takes part in writing a song, Journey take on a different sound. While these songs are not considered anywhere near the best by most fans, they are deep cuts that perhaps diehard fans appreciate. 'Back Talk' has Smith thumping a 'Bo Diddley beat' on the tom-toms. Schon joins in the groove, and Perry does his best to give us a vocal with attitude. It doesn't sound anything like the casual fan's Journey. The focal point is Smith's drums, with Perry's powerful vocals even taking a back seat. Over the years, I would usually skip this track when it came up. But it's grown on me, and I appreciate the skills needed to play it. The track was the B-side to 'Send Her My Love'.

'Frontiers' (Perry, Schon, Cain, Smith) 4:09
We are on our fourth straight minor-key song, which might be a contributing factor to side two's reputation as a bit of a downer. This track has a lurching beat, very 1980s in style, and would not be out of place on Phil Collins' *Face Value*. The lyrics sound like a warning about technology and a changing culture, with a chorus that brings a bit of optimism: 'Out on the border of a changing skyline, we put hope in front of fear. And all the heroes have gone east of Eden. We all need new frontiers'. The keyboards sound a bit dated to the modern ear, but 'Frontiers' is easy to sing along with, thanks to Perry; he showcases a spectacular duet with himself in the fadeout. This title track is an underappreciated gem that didn't make it onto many concert setlists.

'Rubicon' (Perry, Schon, Cain) 4:17
The guitar-driven melody, the shifts in tempo and key, Schon's strong but not overpowering solo, his ornamental guitar flourishes, and Perry's impressive

voice make this a keeper. The message is positive, if a bit earnest. When Perry begins singing, one gets the sense of hearing an Elvis Presley tune with a melodic rock arrangement. The words could have been fished out of Cain's notebooks. In 'Frontiers', we heard the 'east of Eden' metaphor for banished heroes, and here we have the line, 'Make your move across the Rubicon', which is a reference to the river that Caesar, with his army in tow, risked his life to cross, a capital offense for any Roman general to do during the Roman Republic. As a general moral, it is sometimes worth acting on a momentous decision, no matter the consequences. Songs like 'Rubicon' are part of an increasingly common theme in Journey's music: self-help or self-improvement. We are going to be hearing many more of these as we progress through the catalog. Unfortunately, they won't be as musically interesting as this one. 'Rubicon' was the B-side to 'After The Fall'.

Related Tracks
'Ask The Lonely' (Perry, Cain) 3:53
One of the two songs booted off *Frontiers*, this by-the-numbers love song is dripping with Perry's sentiment about coming back from heartbreak. This is a keyboard-driven rocker with excellent harmonies from the band, including a post-bridge a cappella moment. It's a fine song that would have made *Frontiers* an even bigger success. If it and 'Only The Young' had remained on the album, it might have passed *Escape* in sales and popularity.

Instead, the track was included in the December 1983 soundtrack to *Two Of A Kind*, a movie starring John Travolta and Olivia Newton-John. 'Ask The Lonely' was released as a single in Japan (with the B-side 'Troubled Child', the song that replaced 'Ask The Lonely' on *Frontiers*). While it did not chart on the *Billboard* Hot 100, it did, like 'Stone In Love' before it, climb the Mainstream Rock Airplay chart, peaking at number three in January 1984 and lasting for 12 weeks. The song is on *Greatest Hits* and *Time^3*.

'Only The Young' (Perry, Cain, Schon) 4:16
Like 'Ask The Lonely', 'Only The Young' was removed from *Frontiers* only to become one of the staples of Journey's concerts. It features a popular audience sing-along chorus: 'Only the young can say, they're free to fly away, sharing the same desire, burning like wildfire'.

As told in Cain's memoir and the *Time^3* liner notes, Kenny Sykaluk, a 16-year-old battling cystic fibrosis, received a visit from his favorite band via the Make-A-Wish Foundation. They came to Cleveland, Ohio, where Kenny was receiving treatment. Among the gifts the band brought him was a Walkman with a cassette of 'Only The Young'. He was the first person outside of Journey to hear the track. It was an affecting moment for all involved. Kenny died the next day. The song would be a permanent fixture on Journey setlists, starting with the *Raised On Radio* tour, where it served as the raucous opener.

'Only The Young' was included on the soundtrack for the film *Vision Quest* in 1985. Released as a single in January 1985 and peaking on the *Billboard* Hot 100 in March 1985 at number nine, the song stayed on the chart for 16 weeks. It also cruised up the Mainstream Rock Airplay chart, peaking at number three and lasting for 12 weeks. The B-side was another track from the movie by Sammy Hagar, 'I'll Fall In Love Again'. 'Only The Young' is the first track on *Greatest Hits* and is included on *Time^3*.

'Liberty' (Schon, Perry, Cain) 2:53

Other songs were put on tape in 1983 that did not make it onto any albums. This short, moving psalm to freedom features Schon toying with country sounds. His guitar, tuned to sound like a hill country dulcimer, keeps it all low-key. There are no over-the-top rock moments here. While there is a bit too much echo in the vocal track, perhaps intended to sound like Perry singing from a perch in the Rockies, he brings gravitas to the lyrics: 'We all agree, we live to be free. They can't tell us, they can't tell us how to be. We, we all agree, you individually, we the people, share the power, hold the key'. While it borders on the political, it is generic enough to fit anyone's views. This song deserves a second verse and a rhythm section. 'Liberty' is included on *Time^3*.

'All That Really Matters' (Schon, Cain) 3:55

Jonathan Cain delivers lead vocals on this song, recorded during the *Frontiers* sessions but not intended for the album. The synthesized bass riff is the epitome of 1983 pop music, like a milquetoast knockoff of David Bowie's 'Modern Love'. Smith gamely lays down the beat, and Cain does a decent job of singing his own lyrics. While this doesn't sound much like Journey, structurally, it serves as a window. Cain sings the verses in E minor before moving into major chords for the chorus, in keeping with the pessimistic verses about technology and powers that try to control us. The brighter chorus shifts the focus to Cain and his love interest, who are 'all that really matters'. Schon's solo is serviceable but doesn't shake the malaise. The track was never released and is included on *Time^3*.

If you'd like to hear another Cain composition from that era, check out 'Allies' by Heart from their 1983 album *Passionworks*. Led by the piano, 'Allies' has classic Cain lyrics with big choruses and plenty of metaphors. It has a marching beat, so it can feel like it is plodding along, but the piano passages are quite nice. If Steve Perry isn't available to lend a powerful voice, you could hardly do better than Ann Wilson as your lead singer.

'O Holy Night' (Adolphe Adam) 2:25

Journey formed a fan club, *Journey Force*, in 1983 after the success of *Escape*. Members received an ID card, some merchandise, the newsletter and contest prizes. Ron South, keeper of the Journey superfan blog *Wheel In The Sky* (see the 'Bibliography and Websites' appendix), landed a prize for one of those giveaways and received a cassette of this song. Composed in 1847 by Adolphe Adam as an accompaniment to the French poem 'Cantique De Noël', it became an instantly popular melody. While translated into English as 'O Holy Night', this version is an instrumental performed by Neal Schon and Jonathan Cain. If you can find a recording, it is worth a listen. Schon would play another instrumental Christmas song, 'O Come, O Come Emmanuel', accompanied by and arranged by Cain, for 1998's *Merry Axemas, Vol. 2 – More Guitars For Christmas*, featuring various guitarists performing holiday favorites. For guitar fans, finding this album and *Merry Axemas – A Guitar Christmas* is worth the effort.

'Separate Ways (Worlds Apart) [Bryce Miller/Alloy Tracks Remix]' (Perry, Cain) 2:45
'Separate Ways (Worlds Apart) [Extended Remix With Steve Perry]' (Perry, Cain) 3:17
In 2022, a remix of the song by Bryce Miller and Alloy Tracks was used for the Netflix series *Stranger Things*. Once Steve Perry heard it, he worked with them on an extended remix. Both tracks are on the album *Stranger Things: Soundtrack From The Netflix Series, Season 4*. They are both atmospheric and haunting, serving as great showcases for the original music. The shorter remix and the original song briefly charted on the *Billboard* Hot Rock Songs in July 2022.

'Only The Young [Steve Perry/Bryce Miller Remix]' (Perry, Cain, Schon) 3:35
Perry had so much fun working on the extended remix of 'Separate Ways' that he and Miller created a version of 'Only The Young'. It keeps the stylistic approach taken with 'Separate Ways', but other than that, it doesn't add much. Still, it's a laid-back soundscape of a good song and worth a listen.

Released in October 2023, the remix was pressed on a 7" vinyl record (33 1/3 RPM) and tucked into the 40th anniversary vinyl LP release of *Frontiers*, which Steve Perry remastered. The single includes 'Separate Ways (Worlds Apart) [Extended Remix]', and on the B-side, the original singles 'Only The Young' and 'Ask The Lonely'. For Journey collectors, it's a must-have.

Raised On Radio (1986)

Personnel:
Jonathan Cain: keyboards, vocals, DMX programming
Steve Perry: vocals
Neal Schon: guitars, Kurzweil keyboard synth, vocals
Randy Jackson: bass, vocals
Bob Glaub: bass
Dan Hull: sax, harp
Mike Baird: drums
Larrie Londin: drums
Steve Smith: drums
Steve Minkins: additional percussion
Megan Clearmountain: special effects
Produced by Steve Perry
Associate producer and engineer: Jim Gaines
Assistant Engineer: Robert Missbach
Recorded at Plant Studios, Sausalito, California, and Fantasy Studios, Berkeley, California
Mixed by Bob Clearmountain at Bearsville Studios, Bearsville, New York, and Power Station, New York
Second engineers: Mark McKenna, Steve Rinkoff
Release date: 27 May 1986
Highest chart position: US: 34; 2x Platinum Certified
Running time: 44:13

When the *Escape* tour ended, the band were tired. Herbie was ready for them to begin working on the next album, *Freedom*, but it was clear that, to varying degrees, the relentless schedule was taking a toll on each of them. Steve Perry was itching to follow in Schon's footsteps and do his own thing – work on his vision for an album outside of Journey. Schon and Valory had gone through divorces. Steve Smith's wife and infant child had joined the band on the road. They needed some downtime. Yet, being musicians, there is only so much downtime you can have before the need to create comes roaring back.

Schon, specifically, never really takes time off. He seems to always have a guitar with him. He's done a lot of guest session work on various albums, such as his two records with Jan Hammer. During the *Departures* tour, on a free night on the road in Chicago, he went to a blues club and wound up on stage with Buddy Guy – the man is always playing.

During the gap between *Frontiers* and what would become *Raised On Radio*, Schon recorded a song for the soundtrack to the film *Teachers*, with vocalist Eric Martin (who would later front Mr. Big) on the song 'I Can't Stop The Fire'. He also joined up with singer Sammy Hagar, bassist Kenny Aaronson and former Santana bandmate Michael Shrieve to form HSAS. They released *Through The Fire*, which rode the charts through the spring and summer of 1984. Schon sounds great on the album, and he co-wrote most of the tracks with Hagar.

During the hiatus after the *Escape* tour, Steve Smith recorded the eponymous debut album with his band Vital Information, performing instrumental jazz and fusion. The band toured and released a second album in 1984, *Orion*. That's not much of a break from work.

The biggest musical release by an individual band member was *Street Talk*. Steve Perry's solo effort is popular for its hits 'Oh, Sherrie' and 'Foolish Heart'. It spent over a year on the *Billboard* 200, beginning in late April 1984, peaking at number 12. It brought new fans and even more name recognition for the already popular singer. Armed with this success, when he finally agreed to return to Journey for their next album, he had even more power as the de facto leader of the band.

The band supposedly had creative control over their music, but it was within the confines of Herbie Herbert's vision and, with *Frontiers*, the opinions of the record label's AOR man. Herbie's plan for the next album, to be called *Freedom*, would involve either the traditional scarab, phoenix wings and planet on its cover or the Jim Welch 'Elmo' alien motif. That is, it would follow Herbie's desire to have any albums be easily recognized as Journey by the music-buying public when scanning the shelves. However, Steve Perry had other ideas, and they weren't limited to the cover design and album title.

After Perry's success with *Street Talk*, where he enjoyed creative control, he felt emboldened to take on Herbie Herbert directly. Perry stipulated that to return to the band after *Frontiers* and work on a new album, Herbie would have to relinquish his power to make decisions for the band. Continuing without Perry seemed impossible. The six owners of Nightmare (the band members and Herbie) voted, with Herbie sealing his fate with the deciding vote in favor of Perry's terms. Out of this came a new business entity, Elmo Partners, named for that alien head on the cover of *Frontiers*, as a partnership of Perry, Schon and Cain. Elmo Partners replaced Nightmare as the business controlling Journey.

With Perry holding the reins, one of the first things to change was the new album title. *Freedom* would become *Raised On Radio* as Perry's homage to his family. His stepfather operated a radio station in Hanford, California. The radio station featured an Art Deco design, which Perry wanted for the album cover. After declining concepts from a few artists, including Mouse, they asked the artist Prairie Prince, drummer for The Tubes (and Journey during their earliest pre-recording days), to pitch ideas. He and his artistic partner, Michael Cotten, depicted a lone Art Deco-styled radio station in a valley with two radio towers on either side and blue electricity lines connecting them. The call letters on the building's exterior are 'JRNY'.

Perry chose himself to replace Kevin Elson and Mike Stone as producers. Jim Gaines served as an associate producer. He didn't stop there with personnel changes either. He planned to let Ross Valory go, but the bassist quit after a few days of recording when he sensed the new musical direction would be more like *Street Talk* than *Escape*. Bob Glaub replaced Valory and performed on three tracks before Randy Jackson, later famous as one of the judges on *American Idol*, came aboard as the bassist. Jackson, you'll recall, played bass on 'After The Fall' on *Frontiers*.

Meanwhile, Steve Smith had not been brought into the songwriting process as had been the case to this point. Demos of the songs were made with programmed drums – something Perry embraced from his Street Talk experience – and Smith was asked to program his ideas rather than actually play them. To ask a Berkeley-trained musician to do something like this might be considered disrespectful but Smith did work on the three tracks that featured Bob Glaub on bass. He lasted a couple of months before Perry replaced him with session drummer Larrie Londin, known more for his work in country music. While he recorded the rest of the album, Londin did not go on tour with the band. Mike Baird served as drummer during the *Raised On Radio* tour.

Personal turmoil continued to affect Journey, prolonging the album's recording schedule. Cain's marriage ended, as did Perry's long-time relationship with Sherrie Swafford. These events would inspire a couple of tracks, one of which would become a hit. Furthermore, Perry lost his mother to cancer in December 1985 during the recording of the album. *Raised On Radio* was dedicated to her, along with a few other people, including Kenny Sykaluk (see 'Only The Young' under *Frontiers*).

They were forced to move recording locations when the owner of Plant Studios was arrested for distributing drugs from the site. Journey's tapes were confiscated, and by the time they moved to Fantasy Studios in Berkeley, they had lost nearly a month. With these personal, interpersonal, professional, legal and creative differences mounting, it is a wonder they completed *Raised On Radio*.

Based on the photos throughout the album, Journey (Elmo Partners) were a trio with a studio musician rhythm section. *Raised On Radio* is the final record from the pinnacle of Journey's classic era. We will get to *Trial By Fire* soon, but that album, even with the original lineup, was by a band much changed by time and broken relationships.

Unless specified, the bassist is Randy Jackson and the drummer is Larrie Londin.

'Girl Can't Help It' (Perry, Cain, Schon) 3:50
Opening with keyboards and Randy Jackson's bass, the album tries to begin with a hit song about misaligned lovers, but it isn't without its problems. The echo of 'why' at the end of each verse feels corny, and the ending lines – 'there's a fire in his eyes for you' and 'don't you know she still cries for you' – sound uninspired. The biggest problem, which we will hear a few times on

this record, is the combination of the prominence of the rhythm section and the lack of interest it adds to the songs. Neither Jackson nor Londin do much. The drums have the personality of a metronome. The drum fills, when present, are simple, and in later sections, there are no cymbal additions or extra taps on the tom, to the song's detriment. We take such things for granted with Journey, so when they're missing, it makes the music sound a bit sterile. Schon's solo is also less effective than usual. Yet, the melody is catchy and well-sung, which was enough to make it a top 20 hit.

'Girl Can't Help It' was the third single (with the B-side 'It Could Have Been You') released from the album in August 1986. It peaked at number 17 and spent 14 weeks on the chart, while also hitting number nine on the Mainstream Rock Airplay chart and lasting 18 weeks. The track is on *Greatest Hits*. Take the time to compare this with the 'Live Video Mix' version described in 'Related Tracks'.

'Positive Touch' (Perry, Cain, Schon) 4:17
Here is a bouncy relationship rebound song with Cain's piano and Glaub's bass setting the pace. One of Journey's highest-tempo tunes, it pumps along as Schon supplies some muscular chords to the verses. The chorus, with the band echoing the words 'she' and 'touch', adds to the peppy pop song effect. Schon's solo keeps this from being nothing more than a light 1970s Motown knockoff. He rips through it with some swagger, adding balance to the poppy sensibility. At the 2:30 mark, we get a Dan Hull saxophone sequence that feels almost a decade out of date and has phrases that are like those from Tommy Shaw's *Girls With Guns* or Steve Walsh's *Schemer-Dreamer*. It is fun, but it is hardly ever performed live. Steve Smith plays drums here. 'Positive Touch' did serve as the B-side to 'Why Can't This Night Go On Forever'.

'Suzanne' (Perry, Cain) 3:38
Another up-tempo tune, this opens like Kenny Loggins' 'Danger Zone' or David Bowie's 'Modern Love' with its drum machine beat that continues throughout. Perry's vocals add power to the background vocals in the chorus. It's catchy enough that you've probably found yourself singing 'Suzanne' loudly but forgettable enough that you're mumbling the rest of the lyrics. Schon does add an interesting solo with powerful sustained notes, combating the relentlessly monotonous beat. 'Suzanne' was the second single (with the B-side 'Ask The Lonely'), released in June 1986. It peaked at number 17 and spent 13 weeks on the Hot 100 chart. It managed to climb all the way to number 11 on the Mainstream Rock Airplay chart, lasting for ten weeks.

'Be Good to Yourself' (Perry, Cain, Schon) 3:51
Classic Journey come roaring back here. The instrumental opening is reminiscent of 'Separate Ways', but this quickly settles into a 1980s drum machine beat; luckily, Schon embellishes everything with a ferocious (for this

album) guitar. Cain's percussive piano, along with the soaring, uplifting chorus, pushed this into a staple at Journey concerts. Schon is given over a minute to play out the song with an imaginative solo. It is one of the highlights of the album.

Herbie chose this as the lead single, which, according to him, upset Perry because it sounded too much like a traditional Journey song. Whether that story is true or not, the song does sound like classic Journey and is a fine single to launch the record. Released in April 1986 (with the B-side 'Only The Young'), a month before the album release, it peaked at number nine and spent 15 weeks on the *Billboard* Hot 100 chart. It also hit number two on the Mainstream Rock Airplay chart, lasting for ten weeks. 'Be Good To Yourself' is on *Greatest Hits* and *Time*[3].

'Once You Love Somebody' (Perry, Cain, Schon) 4:40
The star here is Randy Jackson as he plucks, slaps and mutes his bass into a funk beat. The song has a Hall & Oates deep-cut vibe. It's not bold enough to be a hit and not heavy enough to be a classic album cut. It doesn't help that this is yet another 'young hearts in love' lyric. Schon plays a 15-second solo during the bridge, and it feels like a missed opportunity to showcase his ability to play funk. He had done it early in his career, for example, with his work on Betty Davis' 1973 eponymous debut on tracks like 'Walkin' Up The Road' or '...Steppin In Her I. Miller Shoes'. Here, he chooses to play sustained notes to match the emotion of the song, but he doesn't have time to create a real payoff. It's all too short. Why not embrace the style like Jackson does on the bass? The track is also on *Time*[3].

'Happy To Give' (Perry, Cain) 3:50
At the end of the first side, the band finally slow it down with this ballad, but don't expect 'Open Arms' or 'Faithfully'. Keyboard- and vocal-heavy, and for me, not counting 'Homemade Love', this is the first time Perry's singing detracts from the overall effect. He is all sustained vowels, skipping over the emotional power of the words. You may feel differently about this, but I am unmoved by this track. Cain's keyboards, including the final synthesized horn fanfares, haven't aged well. No one is credited on bass; it seems to be provided by the keyboards. At the end of the track, during the fade, you get the sense that the song was about to shift gears, but they decided to pull it back, leaving that territory unexplored. Per the *Time*[3] liner notes, Perry recorded the song multiple times, trying to get it done to his satisfaction. One wonders if he was truly happy with this result. 'Happy To Give' is on *Time*[3] and was included on the soundtrack to the 1987 surfing film *North Shore*.

'Raised On Radio' (Perry, Cain, Schon) 3:49
Dan Hull takes us through a bluesy intro on the harmonica before Schon joins in with a crunchy riff. The title track is a paean to the music of the band

members' childhoods. The lyrics are song titles, artist names and words from other songs, all mashed into a rollicking remembrance of the good old days of AM radio rock 'n' roll. The verses are clever, and Perry's passion shines through. Yet, the artificiality of the beat undermines the rock 'n' roll credibility the song needs. This should be a classic and part of the core repertoire. The chorus is infectious, and while Schon's solos don't push the envelope, his guitar does supply some backbone throughout. Then, the ending stumbles its way to silence. This is a good song, but it should have been a great song. Dan Hull also plays saxophone on this track. 'Raised On Radio' got some chart love, spending five weeks on the Mainstream Rock Airplay chart, peaking at number 27.

'I'll Be Alright Without You' (Perry, Cain, Schon) 4:49
What we have here is a fine adult contemporary tune that could have come from any of a dozen musical acts from the late 1970s to the mid-1980s. Even Perry's voice and Schon's guitar do not separate it from the pack of generic, bland, easy-listening works that appear on the pop charts. That is not to say it is bad. For what it is intended to be, a lament about a breakup, it's decent enough. With nearly two minutes to go on the track, Schon plays an extended coda worthy of the smooth jazz of the era.

Despite my complaints, it was a hit, reaching number 14 on the *Billboard* Hot 100. Journey released this as the fourth single (with the B-side 'The Eyes Of A Woman') in December 1986. It showed remarkable staying power thanks to its broad appeal, lingering on the chart for 21 weeks and finding a deserved place on *Greatest Hits*. That broad appeal is reflected in its genre chart performance, where it hit number seven on the Adult Contemporary chart, hanging on for 19 weeks and peaking at number 26 during a six-week run on the Mainstream Rock Airplay chart. Be sure to compare this with the 'Live Video Mix' version described in 'Related Tracks' below.

'It Could Have Been You' (Perry, Cain, Schon) 3:37
Schon does his best to inject life into yet another 'what could've been' song of people unlucky in love. Jackson's bass finds a solid line to complement Schon's guitars (and Schon has an overdubbed solo, too). None of it is very memorable, though. When Cain inserts some synthesized ornamentation, it sounds tacked on. Perry comes across as bored, or at least not that into it. There is a sense that the band are going through the motions. When compared to their best songs, it all feels forced and inauthentic here. Journey, up to this point, have been quite good at making the listener feel the heartache in these types of songs. For me, it's missing here. This track was the B-side to 'Girl Can't Help It'.

'The Eyes Of A Woman' (Perry, Cain, Schon) 4:32
While this comes across squarely as another adult contemporary tune, there are a few things that make it a more interesting listen. The lyrics aren't much.

They consist of a string of metaphors about being hypnotized and fascinated by a woman's eyes, but at least we get a respite from the broken-hearted breakup songs. The tempo is faster than 'It Could Have Been You' but is still deliberate and controlled. Smith has drum duty here, and his presence is heard in the simple fills he does during the transitions. Glaub's bass thumps along without intruding, matching Smith during those same transitions. Schon gets to play both guitar synthesizer and keyboard synthesizer on this track, including an ultramodern (in 1985) Kurzweil. It borders on experimental, which Journey used to do on one or two tracks per album. Perry's vocals and the arrangement of the backing vocals do justice to this lovely track. The song was the B-side to 'I'll Be Alright Without You' and is on *Time³*.

'Why Can't This Night Go On Forever' (Perry, Cain) 3:41
Since the one-two punch of 'Open Arms' and 'Faithfully' on *Escape* and *Frontiers*, respectively, Jonathan Cain gets at least one piano-driven ballad on each album. The opening melody feels like a hybrid of those songs. Cain admits he was writing this with the concert audience in mind. One can imagine this being performed toward the end of the show, perhaps as an encore. While it was performed at a few shows during the *Raised On Radio* tour, it's tough to shoehorn in yet another ballad when you have to play the big ones – it never caught on. Perry sings this with more conviction than some of the others on this album, but the song doesn't lend itself to a crowd singalong. This was the fifth single (with the B-side 'Positive Touch'), released in April 1987, nearly a year after the album came out. It peaked at number 60 and spent 12 weeks on the Hot 100 chart while also spending six weeks on the Adult Contemporary chart, peaking at number 24. The song is included on *Time³*.

Related Tracks
'With A Tear' (Schon, Perry, Cain) 3:25
From the editing room leftovers of *Raised On Radio* comes this instrumental track, completed by Schon and Cain in 1992 and included on *Time³*. Guitar virtuoso fans will find plenty to love as Schon delivers a fine Satriani-style tune. He's not shredding; rather, the guitar is replacing the vocalist to drive and enrich the melody. It is a satisfying way to spend three and a half minutes. This would fit neatly on a Schon solo recording.

'Into Your Arms' (Schon, Perry, Cain) 4:08
Another outcast from the *Raised On Radio* studio time, this sounds like another guitar virtuoso track but with more prominent keyboards and bass. For me, this has the feel of an instrumental track with vocals removed, while 'With A Tear' feels like it was intended to be a guitar-driven instrumental. 'Into Your Arms' is still an interesting track, and Schon gives it some much-needed energy as it progresses. This is also on *Time³*.

'Girl Can't Help It [Live Video Mix]' (Perry, Cain, Schon) 4:17
This concert audio was recorded at the Calaveras County Fairgrounds in Angels Camp, California, on 23 August 1986, the first show of the tour. What a difference a live performance makes for this track. It still suffers from its relentless, unchanging beat, but this is overshadowed by a terrific performance from Perry and the backing vocalists. The synthesized horn fanfare even sounds reasonable. Schon's first bridge solo is intentionally inert, but the next solo sounds fiery and angry. This is a bonus track on the CD release of *Raised On Radio* and was included on *Time³*.

'I'll Be Alright Without You [Live Video Mix]' (Perry, Cain, Schon) 5:01
The live setting improves this track, too, though not as successfully as with 'Girl Can't Help It'. Mike Baird, hired to play drums on the tour, does fine, but Randy Jackson's performance is top shelf. His bass playing pumps life into this somewhat dull track. Likewise, Steve Perry sounds invested here, bringing that powerful voice to bear on the emotional content of the lyrics, something that, to me, was lacking in the studio cut. The backing vocals are solid, and Schon flexes a little towards the end of his solo. This is a far better listen than the album cut. This concert audio was captured at one of the Atlanta, Georgia, shows on 18-19 November 1986. This was included as a bonus track on the CD release of *Raised On Radio* and was included on *Time³*.

Journey's Hiatus (1987-1995)

The *Raised On Radio* tour kicked off in August 1986 in California, with Mike Baird seated on the drum throne. They toured the mainland United States into January 1987, including three shows in Honolulu, before closing out the tour in Anchorage, Alaska. Journey's final live show with Steve Perry as the lead singer was on 1 February 1987. Except for one brief appearance, Journey's nearly decade-long hiatus had begun.

The band members and Herbie Herbert kept busy, though. Here's a short rundown of the music created by the band during this period. Because these are not formally part of Journey's output, they are not covered in detail here.

Jonathan Cain had written and performed a couple of songs, including the hit 'Working Class Man' a few years earlier with Jimmy Barnes, one of the biggest artists in Australia. Now, with Journey on a break, he helped Barnes create and record the album *Freight Train Heart*. Neal Schon and Randy Jackson also appear on the record.

In the late 1980s, Cain bumped into John Waite, and they formed a new band with Neal Schon. They added ex-Babys and future Styx bassist Ricky Phillips and the energetic young session drummer Deen Castronovo. Bad English were born. Their debut, *Bad English*, was released in 1989 and included the Diane Warren ballad 'When I See You Smile'. John Waite wanted to record it despite the objections of his bandmates. Good thing he did. It went to number one on the charts and helped Bad English sell records and concert tickets, though fans were confused by this hard rock band that they only knew from that one sappy ballad. A second album, *Backlash*, came out in 1991 but barely charted, and everyone moved on to other opportunities.

Schon released a couple of solo instrumental efforts – *Late Nite* (1989) and *Beyond The Thunder* (1995). The latter album was released on Higher Octave Records, known for their house style of smooth, laid-back, light jazz. Schon can play anything, and here he is joined by Cain on keyboards. It's a beautiful record.

However, the guitarist hadn't gone completely soft. After Bad English, he brought Castronovo with him to join forces with the guitar-playing Gioeli brothers, Johnny and Joey. They added journeyman bassist Todd Jensen (who will become a working member of Journey in the distant future) and called themselves Hardline. The one album that Schon recorded with them is representative of late 1980s/early 1990s hard rock, with its blend of lyrical machismo, melodic hooks and power chords. Schon does plenty of flexing. For this reason, it is a guilty pleasure of mine and worth a listen. The one minor hit from the album, 'Hot Cherie', is as good as anything from the hair metal era, though a couple of years too late for that genre's heyday.

Schon was involved in so many things that it can be tedious to track. He did guest appearances for Glen Burtnick, Carmen Appice, and ex-Toto singer Fergie Frederiksen. He performed on two tracks on Paul Rodgers' 1993 *Muddy Water Blues: A Tribute To Muddy Waters*. Then, that same year, he brought Castronovo and Jensen with him to record Rodgers' live EP, *The Hendrix Set,* on 4 July in Florida.

Cain, too, went into his studio and recorded a couple of solo albums, both released in 1995. *Piano With A View* is the first of a string of 1990s instrumental albums that he recorded for the Higher Octave label. While this record is not rock, it is a fine slice of light instrumental music. The other release is *Back To The Innocence.* According to Cain, he wrote the title song as his musical response to Don Henley's 'The End Of The Innocence', a sentiment with which he didn't agree. Cain sings on this record, which includes a remake of 'Faithfully'. He knows his vocal limitations and doesn't attempt to copy Perry.

What about the dismissed band members? Steve Smith took full advantage of his free time to put out five albums with Vital Information: *Global Beat* (1987), *Fiafiaga* (1988), *Vitalive!* (1991), *Easier Done Than Said* (1992) and *Ray Of Hope* (1996). Smith was also part of the ever-changing lineup of the jazz group Steps Ahead, with whom he recorded three albums: *Live In Tokyo 1986* (1986), *N.Y.C.* (1989) and *Yin-Yang* (1992). Fans of jazz and fusion should explore these albums.

Ross Valory and Steve Smith teamed up with Gregg Rolie to form The Storm, with lead singer Kevin Chalfant and guitarist Josh Ramos. Valory and Chalfant had cut an album in 1985, with Prairie Prince on drums, as The V.U. Their lone album, *Phoenix Rising,* would not be released until 2000. Chalfant, who sounds a bit like Steve Perry, had worked with Rolie to cut the song 'Show Me The Way', which was included on the debut, *The Storm* (1991). The record's biggest hit, reaching number 26, was 'I've Got A Lot To Learn About Love'. The next year, The Storm recorded a second album, *Eye Of The Storm,* without Steve Smith, but the release was delayed until 1995 for various reasons.

Rolie released albums after leaving Journey, but he didn't tour. Those records, *Gregg Rolie* (1985) and *Gringo* (1987), are vintage Rolie and worth tracking down. He also rejoined Santana for a couple of less-than-successful albums: *Shangó* (1982) and *Freedom* (1987).

Even Herbie Herbert got into the artistic side of the business. He made a couple of albums of blues tracks where he sang and played guitar under the pseudonym Sy Klopps, leader of the Sy Klopps Blues Band. Pat Morrow, Herbie's close friend and road manager for Journey, came up with the moniker. The band released two albums: *Walter Ego* (1993) and *Old Blue Eye Is Back* (1995). Among Journey alumni to make appearances are Gregg Rolie, Neal Schon, Ross Valory and Prairie Prince. They're tough to find, but if you're curious about Herbie, check them out.

Besides all the studio work and touring, members of Journey took part in a couple of events during the hiatus, the biggest one being a memorial. Legendary concert promoter Bill Graham died, along with two others, in a helicopter crash in Vallejo, California, late in the evening of 25 October 1991.

By 3 November, a free concert had been arranged in his honor at Golden Gate Park in San Francisco. The concert featured The Grateful Dead and Crosby, Stills, Nash & Young, along with other guests like Jackson Browne, Joe Satriani and Journey. Herbie was able to round up Jonathan Cain, Neal Schon, and Steve Perry to perform a couple of songs. The band didn't sound all that great, and the massive crowd weren't very responsive. Of the 240 minutes or so of the concert's duration, Journey were on stage for about nine minutes. This was not the reunion that everyone wanted.

Besides keeping to himself and appearing in the lackluster performance at the Graham Memorial, Steve Perry worked on a new album. Released in July 1994, *For The Love Of Strange Medicine* took a few months to be certified gold in the United States. Two of the four released singles broke into the Hot 100: 'You Better Wait' peaked at number 29 and 'Missing You' at 74. The album does not compare favorably to *Street Talk*, but Steve Perry fans got some new music. There are three things of significance related to *Strange Medicine*. First, Steve Perry was writing and recording original music again. Second, Steve Perry was touring in support of the album. Third, Steve Perry got to thinking about the boys, so he made a few calls.

Trial By Fire (1996)

Personnel:
Jonathan Cain: keyboards, acoustic guitars, vocals
Steve Perry: lead vocals
Neal Schon: guitars, vocals
Steve Smith: drums
Ross Valory: bass guitar, vocals
David Campbell: string arrangements
Paulinho de Costa: percussion
Produced by Kevin Shirley
Recorded by Kevin Shirley, George Massenburg and Jonathan Cain at The Site, Marin County, California; Wildhorse Studio, Marin County, California; Ocean Way Recorders, Los Angeles
Mixed by Kevin Shirley
Strings recorded by George Massenburg at Skywalker Ranch, Marin Country, California
Release date: 22 October 1996
Highest chart position: US: 23; 1x Platinum Certified
Running time: 01:07:58

As it happened, everyone was interested in getting back together, but they weren't that good at communicating with each other. Would Journey relaunch with a new lead singer? Was Perry willing to work with Valory and Smith? Were they willing to work with Perry again? John Kalodner, the famous A&R man – who is credited on every album with 'John Kalodner: John Kalodner' to signify that he and his work were uniquely valuable – steered the negotiations. When it was done, the five band members who had created *Escape* and *Frontiers* were together again, only this time, without their manager and driving force, Herbie Herbert. At this point in their professional and personal lives, Herbert and Perry could not work together, so Herbie was out as the manager of the band, though he remained a partner in Nightmare. Industry legend Irving Azoff and his agency took over, and John Baruck managed the band directly.

To produce the album, the label recommended South African engineer Kevin Shirley. Nicknamed 'Caveman', Shirley had most recently been working in Australia, where he engineered the Divinyls' album *Underworld* and produced the teenagers of Silverchair for their debut *Frogstomp*. Dealing with a bunch of successful American millionaires would be a different challenge. While he'd engineered big artists like Billy Squier and Rush, this would be his first time working as the producer for an artist this successful.

He was at odds with the band from the outset, demanding rehearsals until they could play the songs live in the studio instead of working and reworking demos and recording bits and pieces and mixing them together.

The band relented, and four months later, the 16 tracks of *Trial By Fire* were completed.

After the album's release, the planned supporting tour did not happen. Steve Perry had injured his hip while hiking and was in pain while recording the record. Doctors recommended surgery to correct the problem. Perry was hesitant to have the surgery right away. Without Perry, the band did not tour. They waited. After a few years, they stopped waiting, and that is a story for the next album.

The cover art for *Trial By Fire* is unlike any other Journey album. The winged scarab appears on a clay amphora on a beach next to a feathered woman with a cat's head. The woman holds a rope that is held at the other end by a large baby lying naked in a wooden boat, which is beached on the shore of the ocean. The sky is a purple sunset with Egyptian libation bearers pouring water down to the earth. The Journey planet, complete with the torus orbital ring, looms large on the horizon. It's all trippy and brought to us by art directors Nancy Donald and David Coleman. Steven Adler is the illustrator. The CD booklet has details of the cover imagery and fashionable band photos throughout.

'Message Of Love' (Perry, Schon, Cain, John Bettis) 5:34
A half-minute intro kicks off the first track, with Schon blazing through a four-second phrase that gives way to Perry delivering an atmospheric, synth-backed vocalese before Valory and Smith launch the song proper. Perry can still sing, but he's dropped down the scale, and there is a noticeable vocal fry that, in earlier days, he only trotted out for emotional effect. The lyrics, despite help from the venerable songwriter John Bettis, are the usual sentiment of the miserable, lonely person missing someone. The music in the verses is forgettable, but the chorus is catchy. During the opening bars of the bridge, there is a clear call back to 'Separate Ways', which feels both odd and reassuring. Schon's solo and the guitar parts throughout the rest of the song are not up to his usual standards. At the time, though, it was wonderful to hear Journey performing again.

Though it was not a Hot 100 chart hit, it did find its way onto the *Billboard* Mainstream Rock Airplay chart, reaching number 18 in October 1996. By the mid-1990s, singles were rarely released as 45 rpm vinyl. They were replaced by 'maxi-singles'. These mini-CDs held two to four tracks, sometimes including various edits of the main song.

'One More' (Perry, Schon, Cain) 5:27
And then there was track two. A gaudy opening of strings and Perry speaking, 'Wicked prophets ... kill ... speaking His name', at once tell us two things: this is not a lonely-hearts love song, and Journey are willing to take chances again. They haven't used a string orchestra to this extent since *Dream, After Dream*. The song is vague enough to be about any demagogue

in a position of power, whether Western politicians or global terrorists. The idea here is that people are dying because of false prophets, pride, vengeance and anger. Its only religious reference is calling out those who use a deity as a justification for violence. This is a rare theme for Journey. Perry's aching vocal fits this well. Valory adds a bit of personality to his steady playing with a few bass runs during the string-saturated bridge. The strings were overdubbed later, undergirding everything just as Rolie did in the old days with the Hammond B3. It is some fine production work by Kevin Shirley. Schon is given the final minute and a half of the song to play out a solo. He takes full advantage of the opportunity, providing one of the rare guitar-centric moments on the album.

'When You Love A Woman' (Perry, Schon, Cain) 4:06
Here is the one real hit from *Trial By Fire*. It's a by-the-numbers love song, only this time with a happy singer, though it's tough to tell by the slow tempo. It begins with a few lovely bars from Cain on piano. Having heard strings on the hard rock of 'One More', one might be disappointed if they didn't make an appearance on this love song. They show up in time to introduce the bridge before being tastefully doubled by Schon.

'When You Love A Woman' entered the *Billboard* Hot 100 in October 1996 and peaked at number 12. It stayed on the Hot 100 longer than any other Journey hit, 22 weeks, beating out 'Who's Crying Now' and 'I'll Be Alright Without You', each of which lasted 21 weeks. It topped the Adult Contemporary chart for three weeks and stayed there for 35 weeks. Clearly one of Journey's most successful commercial hits, it was added to the *Greatest Hits* when that album was included in the 2006 CD reissues of their catalog. It is not a surprise that this song earned Journey a Grammy nomination, though it is surprising that it was their first nomination.

'If He Should Break Your Heart' (Perry, Schon, Cain) 4:23
The success of the opening three tracks isn't carried over into this forgettable fourth, which could have been another song on *Raised On Radio*. This is a boring, lightweight pop song that returns us to familiar lyric territory. Everyone performs their parts, but the music goes nowhere. Schon heats up toward the end, but it is too late to save it from mediocrity. Released as a single, it didn't chart on the Hot 100. However, it peaked at 21 on the Adult Contemporary chart.

'Forever In Blue' (Perry, Schon, Cain) 3:35
'Forever In Blue' is straight pop and upbeat, but they are not challenging themselves with songs like this. It feels routine. Perry isn't The Voice here. He's merely the lead singer. It's a pleasant spoonful of sugar, easily digested and quickly forgotten. 'Forever In Blue' is a sunny, positive tune about being smitten, which is a respite from the bleakness of some of the following tracks.

'Castles Burning' (Perry, Schon, Cain) 5:58

We finally return to some rock swagger as the track opens with Schon playing over a groove from Smith and Valory. Cain's synthesizer chords at the end of each line of the chorus remind me of early 1980s synthpop. Rolie's Hammond B3 would have been welcomed here. But as the hardest rock track on the record, this is Schon's song to carry, and he does it with some lightning-fast fretwork. Later, he emulates a siren, and while that wears thin after half a dozen times, he keeps it going to the end of the track. At least it fits the fiery metaphor.

The song is about the ending of a relationship between Jimmy and an unnamed woman. The lyrics convey allusions to violence and flames. There are disturbing moments midway through with a news broadcast and Perry eerily saying, 'You know I love you. You know you're my girl. I'd never hurt you'. After an ominous voice saying, 'All's fair in love and war. But war is hell', Schon's siren calls begin. You won't find Journey getting much thematically darker than this.

'Don't Be Down On Me, Baby' (Perry, Schon, Cain) 4:00

If you only had this song as evidence, you would think someone was deaf if they had declared Steve Perry's voice had seen better days. Perry makes this an authentically soulful ballad as he asks for a little understanding from a disappointed partner. Cain carries the song along with string-accompanied piano. Schon delivers a few heartfelt passages. It's all quite effective. For a slow track, it's a keeper. Unfortunately, this track has never been performed in concert, which is a shame. The current singer, Arnel Pineda, could make this a standard.

'Still She Cries' (Perry, Schon, Cain) 5:03

Opening like a contemporary instrumental track from a mid-1990s Cain album, this settles into a bland, minor-key crooner. Journey rarely sound as bored and uninspired as they do here. When the chorus ends with a slightly rising 'good, good, good', it's easy for your attention to drift. Cain's piano is featured throughout the track, sounding like 'From The First Look' on his 1995 album *Piano With A View*. The strings, which have been unobtrusive and primarily supportive, come through a bit too loud and clichéd as the song reaches its ending. This is not one of their best.

'Colors Of The Spirit' (Perry, Schon, Cain, Bettis) 5:39

When Journey attempt something different, I usually enjoy it. 'Colors Of The Spirit' opens with birdsong, percussion from the revered Paulinho de Costa, a synthesized flute that could easily be mistaken for R. Carlos Nakai and Perry singing, 'We are one, we are one'.

Lyricist John Bettis joins the main songwriting trio again. Bettis, a member of the Songwriters Hall of Fame, has written many hits for a diverse set of acts. He started his career co-writing a string of hits with The Carpenters, including 'Top Of The World'. He wrote 'Human Nature' with Toto's Steve Porcaro, a smash hit from Michael Jackson's *Thriller*. Among many other songs, he wrote the lyrics for Whitney Houston's iconic Olympic theme song, 'One Moment In Time', for which he received one of his two Emmy Awards.

That lyrical magic isn't present on his co-writes here, 'Message Of Love' and 'Colors Of The Spirit', although the meaning of the latter song is a good cosmopolitan sentiment in that we are united regardless of our differences. The verses seem pessimistic when compared to the optimism of the chorus. However, the real problem with the song is the abandonment of the interesting opening music. They do return to it at the end, but the middle does not rise above a hackneyed pop song. There are some positives; for example, Valory's bass is so assertive and important to the tune that it could be mistaken for rhythm guitar. But the bass and Schon's high-speed fretwork aren't enough to save a lackluster, plodding track.

'When I Think Of You' (Perry, Cain) 4:20
If you didn't know it was Journey, you would be forgiven for thinking you had fallen into a Barry Manilow album. The piano is appropriately melodic. The strings make their entrance to emphasize the supposed emotion being communicated, just in case the lyrics aren't clear enough. Schon's routine guitar solo reflects his undoubted boredom with all this. Once again, Journey sound mundane. This is fluff that does not belong on this record. Knowing that this is about Perry's late mother does not excuse its forgettable melody. However, because of its personal importance, they chose this track to be included on the 2011 release *Greatest Hits 2*.

'Easy To Fall' (Perry, Schon, Cain) 5:13
This is another slow one, with the strings present and not a memorable melody to be found. For a band coming off a long hiatus, they sound tired and lacking inspiration. The ballads are as good as their counterparts from *Raised On Radio*, but there are so many of them on this record that it becomes difficult to distinguish them from each other. I recall my early excitement and later disappointment with this album because of the abundance of ballads.

This track channels a country-style Journey, not unlike 'Liberty', though this is much slower and more generic in its meaning. Perry sounds great, but the melody is not up to Journey standards, and the chorus is a slog. Schon takes full advantage of the 30-second bridge, tearing through a solo that comes close to lifting the energy level of all involved. But a restatement of the chorus ends that burst of action. Schon single-handedly keeps this from being tossed onto the growing heap of forgettable ballads.

'Can't Tame The Lion' (Perry, Schon, Cain) 4:30

'Can't Tame The Lion' has an interesting guitar intro with its stuttering staccato phrases. It has all the ingredients of a tight rock track; then it stumbles with an awkward chorus that I cannot imagine singing along with at a show.

The chorus is a repeated 'can't tame the LIE-on', sounding out of place and not anthemic in the least. Yet, while listening to the record, I find this track to be such a welcome break from the endless string-laden slow songs that it stands out. Schon gets plenty of time to play, and at least he sounds engaged. This is the last Journey song to chart on the Mainstream Rock Airplay chart, reaching number 33 in February 1997. From this point, their songs only appear on the Adult Contemporary chart and the short-lived Heritage Rock chart.

'It's Just The Rain' (Perry, Cain) 5:19

Schon has little to do except support the piano chords; near the end, however, he plays a gentle, mesmerizing lead. The rhythm section lays down one of the slowest grooves on the record. Unfortunately, a recording of stormy weather is inserted at the end of the track. It's a literal translation of the chorus: 'It's not the love. It's just the rain'.

'Trial By Fire' (Perry, Schon, Cain) 4:39

On an earlier Journey album, this slow, contemplative track would be a welcome contrast to the hard rock and r&b-influenced bouncy pop of everything else. But the potent impact of this quiet, brooding, slow burn is diminished in a sea of insipid ballads. At least Steve Smith has better things to do here than simply keeping the time, as he's done throughout the rest of the album. *Trial By Fire* represents Smith's weakest work with Journey. But on the album's title track, he experiments with various sounds, and his fills are excellent. This could be because, despite the tune's slow tempo and almost overtly religious lyrics, it is closest stylistically to classic Journey. Replace Perry with Rolie on the microphone and this could've been on *Next*. Perry brings intensity to each line without a hint of artificiality. I believe him when he says that this is 'Just another trial by fire'. This is my favorite track on the album.

'Baby I'm A Leavin' You' (Perry, Schon, Cain) 2:47

The hidden track on the original CD is given full acknowledgement on the cover of the reissue. This track, with its reggae beat, is a shot of variety that this album needs. For about three minutes, Journey perform a simple reggae ditty about a boy breaking up with a girl who might be pushing the relationship 'a bit too fast'. The lyrics are clear, singable, and fun despite the breakup theme. Schon manages to channel a bit of the pioneering guitarist Ernest Ranglin as he keeps those syncopated notes going throughout. The percussion, likely from de Costa, adds flavor. Is it a throwaway track? It was hidden, after all. But it's good to hear the band having a bit of fun. It's too bad they didn't have this playful attitude sprinkled throughout the album.

Related Tracks
'I Can See It In Your Eyes' (Perry, Schon, Cain) 4:12
This was only included in the original release in Japan, though since the 2006 CD reissues, it has been on the album proper as a bonus track. Journey let go with a straight-ahead rocker featuring a fast guitar-driven tempo, Smith riding the cymbal at the end of each bar and supplying some of his good old school fills. They rip through this tune without pretentious strings or heartfelt harmonies. It doesn't really fit with anything else on the album. Given what Journey are about to deliver over the next two decades, 'I Can See It In Your Eyes' provides a glimpse of what a Steve Perry-led rocking Journey might have been.

Arrival (2001)

Personnel:
Steve Augeri: lead vocals
Jonathan Cain: keyboards, background vocals
Deen Castronovo: drums, background vocals
Neal Schon: guitars, background vocals
Ross Valory: bass guitar, background vocals
String arrangements: Jonathan Cain
Produced, recorded and mixed by Kevin Shirley at Avatar Studios, New York City, 'World Gone Wild' and 'Nothin' Comes Close' were recorded at The Plant Studios, Sausalito, California and The Cave, New York City
Engineer: Aya Takemura
Release date: 18 December 2000 (Japan), 3 April 2001 (USA)
Highest chart position: USA: 170
Running time: 1:13:50

The public, the record company and the band were ready for the Journey reunion tour when, suddenly, without explanation, it was cancelled. Perry's hip injury, sustained while on a break during the recording of *Trial By Fire*, made it impossible for him to tour without treatment. Instead of being 'cancelled', the tour was 'postponed'. When a couple of years had passed and there was no movement on whether Perry would or could return, Cain and Schon made the widely unpopular decision of replacing the irreplaceable and getting Journey back on the concert circuit. Was it even Journey without Perry? Smith didn't think so, and he left the band a second time. Now, they needed a singer and a drummer.

For the drums, Schon tapped Deen Castronovo, who had played for both Bad English and Hardline. While not the technician Steve Smith is, Castronovo plays with energy, and, as we will see on several tracks, he is a capable vocalist. Castronovo will be the first to say that he is 'a drummer who sings' rather than 'a singer who drums', which is a phrase that, ironically enough, describes Steve Perry.

For the mic, Journey tapped former Tall Stories vocalist Steve Augeri (aw-jair-ree). After singing and playing guitar for a few bands, culminating in a stint with the pop-metal band Tyketto, Augeri left the music business for a time. He was doing maintenance for a retail clothing chain (The Gap) when he got the call to audition to replace Perry. I was lucky enough to see Tall Stories when they opened for Mr. Big on that band's *Bump Ahead* tour. This was before 'To Be With You' became Mr. Big's monster hit, so the venues were small, holding about 500 people. Augeri was a solid lead singer with a great voice capable of soaring arena rock. When Journey announced in 1998 that he was their new lead singer, my first thought was, 'Seems like a good choice.'

Kevin Shirley continued as the producer on *Arrival*, and the band finished the album in 2000. It was released in Japan first. That was when the band discovered Napster. For those who do not recall, Napster and other applications like it were file-sharing services. You could rip a CD to your computer and upload it to a server, and other people could find it and make a copy on the Napster service. It was a great way for the consumer to save money, but it was at the expense of the music creators. In addition to losing sales revenue, the band received some feedback, and it was not unlike the criticism for *Trial By Fire*. There were too many ballads. If the fans wanted any new music, they preferred rock, which is why *Arrival* has the added recording sessions at The Plant and The Cave.

The album did not appear in the United States until 2001. It did not perform well in either sales or airplay. *Arrival* peaked at number 56 on the *Billboard* Hot 200 chart and lasted a mere six weeks. It spawned two singles, neither of which charted on the *Billboard* Top 100. This commercial mediocrity was new territory for a band that had a huge run of success, even with a near-decade hiatus between their prior two albums. After this chart failure, Columbia Records dropped them.

Arrival's art direction switches from long-time director Jim Welch to David Coleman, who, along with Neal Schon, designed the cover art. The artist, Chris Moore, delivered a scarab with gold filigree wings and lapis lazuli and ruby inlays, looking very much like jewelry. No soaring flights and distant planets are found here. The cover is less symbolic than *Trial By Fire*. The group photos by Marina Chavez show the band at their dapper, leather-clad best. In both photos, they wear black leather, but in one of them, Augeri is wearing red leather pants, which might be the only part of the packaging that holds a message: there's a new singer in town.

'Higher Place' (Schon, Jack Blades) 5:09
Jack Blades, from Night Ranger, Damn Yankees and Shaw Blades, wrote this and three other *Arrival* tracks with Schon and other members of Journey. 'Higher Place' leads off as the best pop-rock tune of *Arrival*'s 16 songs. Blades' fingerprints are all over this to the point where it sounds like an early Night Ranger track, especially in the vocal arrangements.

The last section, where Augeri really shines, includes the band's vocal harmonies, with Augeri's strong lead adding variations to the chorus, all underscored by Schon and the rhythm section. This is one of my favorite post-Perry songs, not because of its originality or profound lyrics but because it has a relentless melodic rock drive. It feels good to listen to.

However, it isn't perfect. The vocals are not as prominent in the mix as they could be, and that makes it difficult to understand the lyrics. Augeri sings clearly enough, but Castronovo, Vallory, and Schon stomp on a few words here and there. Musically, while it's fun, it also doesn't change much over its five-minute duration. They cut nearly a minute for the radio edit.

The song was the first of three tracks released from the album. 'Higher Place' hit the *Billboard* Heritage Rock chart in March 2001, peaking at number 23 and staying on the chart for 11 weeks. It was Journey's second and final song to appear on that chart (see 'Remember Me' in 'Related Tracks' below).

'All The Way' (Taylor Rhodes, Cain, Schon, Augeri) 3:35
The first song to feature an Augeri co-writing credit is a soft rock singalong. It doesn't have a strong hook, and its boy-band vibe certainly wasn't supported by a choreographed dance video. At least one critic made the comparison to N'Sync or New Kids On The Block. Journey were a middle-aged pop-rock outfit approaching their 30th anniversary, not baby-faced vocalists.

After a brief intro, the piano handles melodic duties when Augeri begins singing. Cain's string arrangements are unobtrusive, meaning boring and not memorable. The band appear to be gunning for a big chart hit and creating a new concert mainstay with their new vocalist. They didn't succeed.

'All The Way' spent 13 weeks on the *Billboard* Adult Contemporary chart beginning in April 2001, peaking at number 22 by late May. The single's B-side is an even softer mix without guitar.

'Signs Of Life' (Cain, Elizabeth Cain, Schon) 4:54
One hears enough Cain to know his lyrical handiwork, this time joined by his then-wife, Liz. We are presented with an efficient blend of pop-rock, ready for radio and stage. Yet, ironically, the signs of life aren't present. It isn't discernible from plenty of other adequate songs vying for your time, money and attention. Journey are far too talented to settle for this. This is a mature song about moving on – some claim to hear references to Perry's silence – that has a decent chorus, but musically, it's a bit of a chore to sit through.

Schon plays some licks from 'Who's Cryin' Now', which is both petty and funny and could be interpreted as a swipe at Perry.

'All The Things' (Schon, Cain, Andre Pessis) 4:22
Journey have built a fine collection of pop-metal songs over the years, and 'All The Things' fits the criteria. Schon dominates the tune from the beginning, supplying power chords and little fretwork embellishments at every opportunity. The verses are sung with a melancholy style, moving to a chorus that picks up the pace with heavy support from the guitar. This is a love song, but it's difficult to tell with the grunge-like delivery, which turns out to be rather refreshing. Co-writer Andre Pessis also collaborated on 'Walking Away From The Edge' on the EP *Red 13*.

'Loved By You' (Cain, Kim Tribble, Tammy Hyler) 4:02
It would be over a decade before Jonathan Cain built Addiction Sound Studio in Nashville, and part of his decision to move there after leaving California and selling his Wildhorse Studio was because of the songwriting collaborations he did in Tennessee during this period.

Kim Tribble and Tammy Hyler were respected country songwriters. Tribble had cowritten Mindy McCready's number-one Country song 'Guys Do It All The Time', among many other hits. He co-wrote six songs for *Arrival* and one for *Generations*. He also wrote with Cain for his solo work. Tribble died in 2021. Tammy Hyler has written country hits for Martina McBride and George Strait, among others. This Nashville influence did not turn Journey into a country act. Their involvement was intended to help soften the blow of losing Steve Perry's songwriting skills.

'Loved By You' is a part of the long chain of attempts to recreate the magic of 'Open Arms' and 'Faithfully'. Despite the aid of a couple of Nashville's finest, it falls short of the goal. The song opens with piano and some subtle coloring from the guitar that hints at something exotic happening, but it turns into a vocal, strings and cymbal-saturated banal ballad before long. One of the characteristics of the earlier two hit ballads, aside from the great vocals, is a level of musicality and complexity that makes them so memorable. 'Loved By You' has none of that. The first few seconds of the intro sound promising, and then it turns into background music.

'Livin' To Do' (Schon, Matthew Schon, Cain, Tribble) 6:24
If Journey wanted to do an album full of tracks like this, it might not sell well, but it would be an honest and authentic treasury of what they can do when they abandon commercial considerations. Written by Schon and his father, Matthew, who was losing his battle with cancer, and with help from Cain and Tribble, this introspective, bluesy workout is Journey at their best. Schon begins the song with nearly a minute of reflective playing, transferring his feelings from heart to fingers to strings. Cain adds a soft synthesized pillow of sound for the intro.

Augeri supplies the potency and gravitas these philosophical lyrics require. The song is an aural *memento mori* (Latin for 'remember you are mortal'), that is, a reminder that we aren't here forever.

A bit past the halfway point, Schon begins a minute-long solo. He keeps the notes lengthy and mixes equal parts bravado and anguish. The band's approach normally doesn't allow for this sort of indulgence, and cutting this solo short would have been criminal. After the final soaring chorus, the song downshifts, and as Castronovo and Valory lay down the rhythm, Cain plays a tasteful keyboard solo, with Schon adding layers. The solo sounds like comfortable nostalgia with a few regrets, a winding down towards a well-deserved rest. Schon closes it out with an abbreviated return to his opening. It is such a beautiful song.

In the liner notes, Schon says, 'In loving memory of my Dad, he and his music will live forever inside me. He has reminded me that I have 'Livin' To Do'...'

'World Gone Wild' (Schon, Cain, Blades) 6:00
Our second Blades co-write is another driving rocker with a less memorable melody than 'Higher Place'.

Schon has some fun shredding throughout. This is quite like 'Higher Place' and shares that Night Ranger sound. 'World Gone Wild' is one of the two tracks ('To Be Alive Again' is the other) hastily recorded for addition on the United States release after complaints that the Japan release was too heavy on the ballads. While it rocks, it doesn't leave a lasting impression.

'I Got A Reason' (Schon, Cain, Blades) 4:18
Written by the same songwriters of 'World Gone Wild', this track differs in that it has an upbeat rhythm. The vocal line is classic Jack Blades, with each verse line ending on an extended note. Augeri delivers the lyrics with energy. While Schon's solo isn't all that inspired, he has a few flourishes, notably at the beginning of each chorus and then at the end of the solo, providing some variety.

'With Your Love' (Cain, Elizabeth Cain, Schon) 4:25
Liz Cain joins her husband and Schon for the album's 'wedding' song. This syrupy ballad is earnest in its bid to be performed while a happy couple stand at the altar. The opening line – 'On this day, to be standing here with you. There's no doubt, I know this love is true' – couldn't be more on the nose. Augeri's vocals do not bring anything special that would separate this from any other trite wedding song. I feel like I'm listening to a talented co-worker doing a pretty good karaoke number. As the song crescendos, Schon plays his patented power ballad solos. We've heard it many times by now.

As far as songs for nuptials go, this is as good as any. Journey released this as a single, but it did not make it onto any of the various *Billboard* charts. The single includes a slightly shorter radio edit.

'Lifetime Of Dreams' (Schon, Cain, Tribble) 5:29
Opening like a variation of 'Too Late', with Schon playing little figures after the beat, this settles into ballad territory, but with a welcome emphasis on the guitar. The backing vocals, with their rising 'ahh's, complement a strong lead from Augeri. Schon's first solo starts at 2:52 with some extended notes before he speeds it up. This leads to an interchange (3:35) between Schon and Augeri. Schon has a second solo at 4:13, with Augeri joining in shortly with a refrain that carries on for another half minute. Schon then continues his solo to the end of the track. It's a lyrically simple love song but powerfully delivered. One of the strongest of the Augeri era.

'Live And Breathe' (Augeri, Schon, Cain) 5:14
Recalling the first time I heard this, I thought it was a new Triumph song. Augeri channels Rik Emmett's distinctive tenor. Valory's bass line is more prominent than usual, accompanied by Castronovo's steady drumming, holding Schon in check until the chorus allows for more emphasis on the guitar. The song builds in tension before Schon lets rip at the 3:40 mark.

'Nothin' Comes Close' (Schon, Cain, Augeri) 5:41
The second track to come out of the emergency sessions before the United States release of *Arrival* is this rocker. Schon plays continuously throughout the song's nearly six-minute duration in a preview of 2011's *Eclipse*. Cain's contributions are minimal, with a quiet background synthesizer emulating an organ. Everything here is in service to Schon. The words are innocuous, and the chorus is close to being crowd-ready but ends up a little too wordy: 'I've been around the world, ain't much that I've missed. It doesn't get much better than this. Oh baby, nothing comes close to your kiss'.

It all feels a bit thrown together, but it is worth a listen if you like pop-rock Journey. 'Nothin' Comes Close' is not included on the Japan release.

'To Be Alive Again' (Cain, Augeri, Tribble, Eric Bazilian) 4:21
Cain and Augeri are joined by songwriters Kim Tribble and, from The Hooters, Eric Bazilian. A song of nostalgia, which is a staple of songwriters like Cain and Bazilian, this tune leaps out of the gate with a drum fill, the clack of the piano and power chords from Schon.

Regardless of the lack of any specific Journey characteristics, the song remains a solid rocker with mature self-improvement lyrics about waking up and living with purpose. The band sound like they're enjoying themselves. 'To Be Alive Again' has a catchy hook and moves along at a good pace. Instead of wearing out its welcome, it fades a bit early. The version of this song on the Japan release does carry on for 20 to 25 seconds longer, which brings the song to a more satisfying conclusion.

'Kiss Me Softly' (Schon, Blades, Augeri) 4:47
Synthesizer and piano accents from Cain, laid-back, deceptively masterful guitar from Schon, an effortless, flashy bass line from Valory and a cool jazz beat from Castronovo make Journey at their adult contemporary best. This sounds like an unused track from *Trial By Fire*. 'Kiss Me Softly' is a pop ballad with Augeri in fine voice. It isn't quite yacht rock, but you can hear it in the marina parking lot.

'We Will Meet Again' (Schon, Augeri, Tribble) 5:05
With these sentimental lyrics, I'd swear that Cain was one of the writers, but here, he is limited to providing piano and synthesizers. Augeri sounds good throughout, and the interesting, repeated backing vocals singing 'We will meet again' add to the heartbroken atmosphere of love lost. The lyrics never get too syrupy or maudlin. Schon nails a simple, synth-like solo. Castronovo never relents on the beat, taking the song to a halting, melancholic conclusion.

I'm not one to believe this song is an allusion to Steve Perry, but I could see it if it proved to be true. The themes of missed connections, miscommunications and bad interpretations are all aligned with the band's struggles to stay together. Either way, it is a fine track and is one of my personal favorites on the album and the post-Perry era.

'I'm Not That Way' (Schon, Cain, Augeri, Tribble) 4:23
Not included on the American release, 'I'm Not That Way' is a straight ballad in the vein of Mr. Big's 'To Be With You', complete with the 'he hurt you, but I never will' message, though without the charm or catchy chorus. Still, it is a serviceable ballad in a catalog fully stocked with serviceable ballads. This is on the Japan release only.

Related Tracks
'Remember Me' (Schon, Cain, Blades) 5:29
There were several years between the announcement of new lead singer Augeri and the release of their first full album since *Trial By Fire*. When they pulled Augeri from his maintenance duties at New York City's *Gap* clothing stores, he joined the band in California for some sessions. They ended up recording a few songs, including 'Remember Me'.

A simple guitar phrase introduces the song as the band dramatically belt out 'Remember me' twice before Augeri proceeds to sing a rather boring pop-rock song. As the song heads toward its finish, the piano can finally be heard around the 4:25 mark as Schon takes a breather.

To introduce the new singer, Columbia negotiated its inclusion on the soundtrack to the summer blockbuster movie *Armageddon* (1998). Diane Warren, who wrote Bad English's number-one hit earlier in the decade, also wrote the big hit from this soundtrack, 'I Don't Want To Miss A Thing', performed by Aerosmith. 'Remember Me' was released as a CD single containing three versions: the radio edit, the album cut and an extended version, which is only available on the single. The extended version allows for extra guitar time as the song fades. While it didn't touch the *Billboard* Hot 100, it did spend three weeks in July on *Billboard*'s short-lived Heritage Rock chart, peaking at 39.

Red 13 (2002)

Personnel:
Steve Augeri: lead vocals
Jonathan Cain: keyboards, rhythm guitar, background vocals
Deen Castronovo: drums, percussion, background vocals
Neal Schon: lead and rhythm guitars, background vocals
Ross Valory: bass guitar, background vocals
Produced by Neal Schon and Jonathan Cain
Recorded and mixed at Wildhorse Studio, Novato, California
Engineered by Jonathan Cain
Mixed by Jonathan Cain, Neal Schon and Gary Cirimelli
Mastered by Gary Cirimelli
Release date: 26 November 2002 (Frontiers label release)
Highest chart position: USA: did not chart
Running time: 24:29

Despite being let go by Columbia after nearly three decades, Journey pressed on with personal projects and concert tours with fellow 'heritage' bands like Styx and REO Speedwagon. They also found time to cut loose at Cain's Wildhorse Studio in California, where they recorded this EP. Released in August 2002 on their JourneyMusic label, the disc was sold at the concert merchandise tables and via the band's website. The cover art is centered on a field of black, with 'RED 13 JRNY' in a simple red logo consisting of the '13' in a central target and the words to either side of it as black letters set in solid red bars. It looks like the maximum level of abstraction of the winged scarab. By November, Journey officially released the album via Frontiers, the Italy-based record company that champions new music in the melodic rock genre. The band issued the retail version with a new cover, designed by a fan, artist Christopher Payne, that was more aligned with Journey's usual imagery. A red scarab, feathered wings fully extended, has a star or planet shining brightly above its head. The band name is at the top and the album title is at the bottom, all on a field of black. The effect is fiery – perhaps an unintentional allusion to the story of Icarus, who flew too close to the sun. The EP did not have significant sales and did not chart or produce any hits.

'Intro: Red 13'/'State Of Grace' (Schon, Cain, Augeri) 7:27
The first two minutes of the opener feature the Cain-penned 'Intro: Red 13' with a rapid percussion pattern building with heavy synthesizers and guitar to the point where it sounds like a cut from The Prodigy. Journey have not recorded anything like this for decades. Schon stated that they had no label to answer to, so they would experiment and have fun. This approach created a mixed reaction from fans, with some looking for anything but another radio-ready ballad and others hoping for something reminiscent of their most popular hits.

'State Of Grace' is a minor-key, high-energy rocker. Augeri is clear and easy to understand, as *Red 13*'s sound is far superior to *Arrival*. Oddly, the song's verses are better than the chorus, which decelerates the speed and energy of the track. Schon's guitar is ever present, accenting each line of verse and filling all the gaps. He shreds the solo, but for the first time in a great while, he drifts from the melody and feel of the song. Here, he moves a bit beyond with some fiery playing, which sounds great but doesn't quite fit the tune. In the final 30 seconds of the track, the opening percussion pattern returns and takes us to the end.

'The Time' (Schon, Cain, Augeri, Cirimelli) 6:25
The three songwriters are joined by the creative engineer and synth programmer Gary Cirimelli. Despite the frenetic pace kept up by Schon's guitar, underneath this is a deliberately paced, cerebral love song. Augeri sings with conviction on such lines as 'How long has it been since you felt the love? You gave up on counting days to count the days since you gave up'. Lyrically, this is the best song on the EP.

The chorus has the same style as found on 'We Will Meet Again', only this time, the backing vocals sing, 'All we need is the time'. Valory's melodic bass line propels the song forward. Unfortunately, the entire track is overshadowed by the guitar. At times, it feels like Schon is playing a different song. It's relentless and too prominent, with a garish solo that takes away from the overall power of a song that deserves a better, less intrusive treatment.

'Walking Away From The Edge' (Cain, Schon, Andre Pessis) 6:17
Augeri shows just how strong and well he can sing on this emotional track about recovery. Though no specific addiction is mentioned, it works as a generic tale of being on the edge of self-destruction. Journey don't do many of these introspective works unless it's about lamenting a lost love. The words are full of strong, direct confessions and declarations of responsibility. In the chorus, the line 'Freedom comes day by day till the demons are out of my head' sounds authentic. Unlike 'The Time', Schon contributes an appropriate level of guitar, keeping it low-key and sincere. 'Walking Away From The Edge' was intended for but omitted from *Arrival*. Geoff Tate of Queensrÿche is an uncredited co-writer.

'I Can Breathe' (Schon, Cain, Augeri, Taylor Rhodes) 4:20
The final track is a standard rock workout that continues the run of songs dealing with the general challenges of being an adult, stressed out but hopeful. This also continues a string of fine vocal performances from Augeri and the band, though the chorus can sometimes unintentionally sound like 'I *can't* breathe'.

Taylor Rhodes is a co-writer, as he was on *Arrival* with 'All The Way', which likely places this track as another leftover from that overstuffed record. One could make a credible argument that, had they been selected, these songs would've made *Arrival* a better album.

Generations (2005)

Personnel:
Steve Augeri: lead vocals, acoustic guitar, guitar
Jonathan Cain: keyboards, rhythm guitar, lead and background vocals
Deen Castronovo: drums, percussion, lead and background vocals
Neal Schon: lead and rhythm guitars, lead and background vocals
Ross Valory: bass guitar, lead and background vocals
Produced by Kevin Elson
Recorded by Mike Fraser, assisted by Mike Baden at The Plant Studios, Sausalito, California
Additional recording at Prairie Sun Studios, Cotati, California
Release date: 29 August 2005
Highest chart position: USA: 170
Running time: 1:13:18

Despite being without a label, Journey continued touring. They weren't selling new music, but that catalog of their primary hits still drew respectable crowds. The band, never above doing things for publicity, obtained a star on the Hollywood Walk of Fame. For that event in January 2005, the current lineup was joined by George Tickner, Aynsley Dunbar, Steve Smith, and, in a nice gesture to the band's history, Robert Fleischman. The real surprise, though, was the appearance of Steve Perry. No one was sure he would show. Nothing came of it other than exciting the crowd. He left the event after a short speech and a quick photo. Everyone else attended the after-party, which included Fleischman joining the band to sing 'Wheel In The Sky', his biggest songwriting contribution.

Meanwhile, the band had more touring to do, and they would create another album of original material. Instead of continuing with Frontiers, they went with Sanctuary Records, a subsidiary of BMG. The plan was to include the CD as part of the concert ticket price. CDs were handed out upon entry to the venue. The band hoped that these CDs would count as sales for chart rankings. That approach didn't work, and *Generations* lasted only one week on the *Billboard* Hot 200.

The other problem, though it was not publicly known at the time, was Steve Augeri's struggles with his vocal cords. Hard touring is tough on singers, and when one sings Journey's soaring hits night after night, it takes its toll. It happened to Perry in the past, and it would happen to Arnel Pineda in the future. Augeri didn't possess the same confidence as Perry to declare that he needed a break. The band needed to continue touring, so they accommodated Augeri, including using some pre-recorded vocals. This controversy is described in depth elsewhere (see bibliography), but for our purposes, it helps explain the approach of having everybody take turns at the microphone for this album. It is interesting, and it doesn't always work out so well, but it did reveal the surprisingly strong voice of Deen Castronovo.

The band went back to Kevin Elson, who worked magic for them in the producer's chair back in the early 1980s. It seemed like the perfect setup for a classic album. Yet, *Generations* is an odd duck. The overall sound quality is muted. When Cain's keyboards are not the primary instrument, they are buried in the mix. All too often, Augeri's voice is difficult to hear over the guitar. The rhythm section, while always competent, doesn't sound distinct on this record. It is the only official album that Journey do not mention on their website, and, as of this writing, it is not available on any major streaming services. Augeri is the lead singer unless noted.

The album cover is a star field of dark purple with a winged scarab in the center. The writing on the cover and in the lyrics and liner notes is not the easiest to read when foregrounded by that galactic cloud. The art likely looks better on a larger scale. Craig Howell is the cover artist.

'Faith In The Heartland' (Schon, Cain, Augeri) 6:56
An attempt at a blue-collar anthem starts the album. After a 45-second keyboard opening, Schon launches into this song about staying steady and faithful through all the changes happening to our towns, our jobs and our families. If we just keep our faith and hold fast, everything will be fine.

The band's sheer competency masks some mundane lyrics. Schon's solos can only elevate the work so far. This is a problem that covers a lot of the post-Perry phase of Journey's history. Cain's lyrics tend to be a collection of phrases that circle his main theme. The emotional connection is superficial at best. Perry's lyric writing creates story scenes that bring the feelings to life. His singing style also communicates the emotional weight of the song. Here, Augeri sings the litany of phrases with a bland, repetitive cadence that makes 'Faith In The Heartland' some tough going as it stretches toward seven minutes.

'The Place In Your Heart' (Schon, Cain) 4:23
This is what 'Faith In The Heartland' might have been if it was a bit shorter. This is a by-the-numbers melodic rock tune where Schon and Cain make full use of the 'verse-verse-chorus' and 'bridge with solo' template. Nothing surprises the listener here. Still, it is nice to hear Cain banging on the piano during these higher-tempo rock songs. He takes a back seat quite often on most of the rock tracks, saving his keyboard work for the ballads.

'A Better Life' (Schon, Cain) 5:40
Lead vocals: Deen Castronovo
As noted earlier, Castronovo has described himself as 'a drummer who can sing, not a singer who can drum'. While it is understandable that he doesn't want to sing every song every night, he is a capable vocalist, as he demonstrates in 'A Better Life'.

This is another song about making it through tough times. Here, it's a young married couple of high school sweethearts. This laid-back tune has some fine moments from Schon. Castronovo varies his vocal delivery, which is more in line with Perry's varied style. 'A Better Life' lacks a memorable hook but still deserves a listen.

'Every Generation' (Schon, Cain) 5:55
Lead vocals: Jonathan Cain
The exception to the risk-avoidance rule is here. Plenty of critics pan Cain's vocal work, but he does bring energy to the song. Would this be better with a singer with a wider range? Of course, but it is still an enjoyable track. Lyrically, this is about young people doing what young people will do, whether it is 1974 or 2024. Lines such as 'There's a brand-new face waiting right behind every generation' suggest that today's kids are tomorrow's grumps, so maybe we should lighten up and enjoy the new while cherishing the old. This would be a good re-record with Pineda at the mic.

'Butterfly (She Flies Alone)' (Augeri) 5:59
Steve Augeri has a rare solo writing credit as he takes back the microphone and even plays some acoustic guitar. In this slower song, heavy on piano, Augeri sings of a woman who is trapped in a relationship or situation but is slowly breaking free. The metaphor describes this struggling transition as a butterfly breaking out of its chrysalis. It's leisurely and atmospheric, with some nice touches by Schon and more piano work from Cain.

It lingers a bit too long at six minutes, but it is nice to hear an Augeri contribution.

'Believe' (Augeri, Tommy De Rossi) 5:41
Opening with a stuttering, uplifting melody in A major, with the band led by piano once again, 'Believe' is a healthy, optimistic song about the power of supporting one another. The music during the chorus of 'I believe in you, believe in me' doesn't have as much power as the rest of the track, and towards the song's midpoint, it gets repetitive. The piano-driven melody used during the verses is a potential earworm. One of Schon's strongest solos on this album starts at 2:35 and lasts half a minute. Augeri contributes rhythm guitar.

'Knowing That You Love Me' (Cain) 5:23
Time for the obligatory Cain wedding song. 'Knowing That You Love Me' is a bit different from the usual Cain ballad. While his keyboard is present, he has Schon's six-string taking responsibility for the melody. Augeri's voice rings with strength and dedication. The backing vocalists seem to take on the role of a gospel choir in the choruses, singing, 'You lift me up, if I should fall', along with Augeri. It's a nice touch that adds to the gravitas despite the usual love song cliches. For a post-Perry ballad, it rises slightly above its competition.

'Out Of Harm's Way' (Schon, Cain) 5:16

'Out Of Harm's Way' allows Schon to flex his muscles. The song is about a good, down-on-his-luck, working-class young man who has no choice but to join the military. He is sent to war but has his faith to comfort him; there is even a verse about his trauma once he returns home. This is some heavy topical content tucked inside a driving rock beat, with Schon cutting loose at every opportunity. Augeri, with strong backing vocals from Castronovo, brings the rock swagger. This song could use some growling to match the furious guitar work.

The chorus is vague and has little to do with the specific story being told in the verses. The song sounds good and raucous, and, in my opinion, with a stronger chorus, this could be a concert favorite.

'In Self-Defense' (Schon, Cain, Perry) 3:12
Lead vocal: Neal Schon

How on earth did a Steve Perry co-write find its way onto *Generations*? Originally intended as a Journey song, Neal Schon and Jan Hammer put it on their second collaboration, *Here To Stay*, in 1982, titling it 'Self Defense'. A few members of Journey joined the recording of that track. Ross Valory stood in on bass, replacing Colin Hodgkinson, and Steve Smith played drums. Steve Perry joined, too, providing some of his distinctive backing vocals while holding back from overshadowing Schon, who sings and shreds his way through the three-minute running time.

When it came time to select a song for Schon to sing on *Generations*, 'Self Defense' was made an official Journey tune. The remake is practically a note-for-note copy despite not having Perry to add color. Listening to this, either the original or the remake, I'm reminded of early Van Halen, who seems to serve as inspiration. Considering they toured together quite a bit in the late 1970s, it makes sense. The backing vocals on the remake remind me of Michael Anthony's high tenor.

'Better Together' (Schon, Cain, Augeri) 5:08

Another pop metal rocker, this is reminiscent of the big hair tunes of the late 1980s. Journey can generate these nearly as easily as a ballad, and listening to Schon go off can be fun, but nothing distinguishes this track from dozens of others recorded by lesser bands nearly two decades earlier. The lyrics are straight out of the hard rock handbook: 'Knowing I'll be there if you should fall, yeah, we're better together.' I don't mind cliché-filled songs if there is something to raise them up a notch. Despite Schon's best efforts, that something is not here.

'Gone Crazy' (Schon, Amber Schon, Cain, Tribble) 4:07
Lead vocal: Ross Valory

Everyone gets at least one track to sing lead vocals, and the notorious 'Gone Crazy' gives us the blustery growl of Ross Valory. The song rarely receives any love, but it has a few redeeming qualities. First, the boogie laid down by these guys is energetic and fun. Schon is in his element when he gets to let go. The backing vocals provide some needed assistance. Valory doesn't have any range to speak of, but he does have a growl reminiscent of ZZ Top's Billy Gibbons. Amber Schon, Neal's wife at the time, and Kim Tribble contributed lyrics. It's fun, but if you prefer your Journey melodic and mellifluous, you'll likely skip this.

'Beyond The Clouds' (Schon, Augeri) 6:57
'Beyond The Clouds' is slow and sounds like a lament, but it's sung in a major key. There's hope in the lyrics despite the allusions to grief. Augeri has said this was inspired by the events of 9/11, though the lyrics do not mention anything specific to tie it to that tragedy.

Closing out the final two minutes, Schon's gentle, soulful guitar, along with Cain's keyboards, sounds like they could have been lifted from either of their solo 1990s smooth jazz instrumental albums. They've created a song with some lovely parts, but somewhere along its interminable playing time, your attention might drift. This is Journey as background music.

Related Tracks
'Never Too Late' (Remixed Version) (Schon, Cain, Blades) 5:00
Lead vocal: Deen Castronovo
This Sanctuary Records bonus track is a remix used for Frontiers Records' European release of *Generations*. Co-written by Schon, Cain and Jack Blades, 'Never Too Late' is a fast-paced rocker with Cain on rhythm guitar. Castronovo's vocals add some personality despite occasional tentativeness. Lyrically, it resembles an advertisement for marriage counseling while maintaining a positive message. Schon delivers two solos, the second with a rawer feel. Overall, it's a solid rock track that stands out thanks to Castronovo's vocals.

'Pride Of The Family' (Cain) 4:00
Lead vocal: Jonathan Cain
Included on the Japan release of *Generations*, 'Pride Of The Family' is Cain's song about a father's daughter growing up rapidly. It isn't difficult to see that he is singing about his own family and his daughter, Madison.

That beautiful paternal sentiment is boosted by some subtle guitar from Schon. His little embellishments are clever and effective. The acoustic guitar throughout the song turns this into something less dramatic than a piano-based ballad, which is exactly what is needed for a love song from a father to his daughter. Cain's voice works well, and while it doesn't sound like traditional Journey, it's time to declare, after two albums and an EP without Perry, that maybe new traditions are underway.

Revelation (2008)

Personnel:
Jonathan Cain: keyboards, backing vocals
Deen Castronovo: drums, percussion, vocals
Arnel Pineda: lead vocals
Neal Schon: all guitars, backing vocals
Ross Valory: bass, backing vocals
Produced by Kevin Shirley
Recorded at The Plant, Sausalito, California
Engineer: John Neff
Release date: 3 June 2008
Highest chart position: USA: 5; Platinum Certified
Running time: 1:44:50

Journey found themselves in a controversy while on tour with Def Leppard after recording *Generations*. Credible accusations of lip-syncing by Augeri led to his departure from the tour, purportedly due to a throat ailment. Enter the journeyman vocalist Jeff Scott Soto, who had worked with Schon on Soul SirkUS, a side project from an abandoned collaboration with Sammy Hagar. Soto finished the tour with the band, but instead of being the new official lead singer, he was let go while the band continued searching for their next vocalist.

As these events unfolded, the next wave of Journey's participation in American pop culture was about to launch. The songwriters, including Steve Perry, approved the use of 'Don't Stop Believin'' in the finale of the HBO hit show, *The Sopranos*. In the scene, Tony Soprano selects the song from a diner's table-side jukebox. As the song plays, members of Tony's family arrive, other patrons come and go and an uneasy tension builds. There's a close-up of Tony's face, and as Perry sings 'Don't stop', viewers are greeted by a black screen and total silence. The popularity of the show, combined with this song to set up this enigmatic ending, had people streaming and downloading the track.

Then, the use of the song in the hit television musical series *Glee* and other media led to *Greatest Hits* returning to the *Billboard* charts. Journey saw this as an opportunity and needed a singer to capitalize on it.

They turned to a singer from Virginia, Jeremey Hunsicker, based on a recommendation from Cain's daughter, Madison. After watching YouTube videos and attending a live performance of Hunsicker's Journey tribute band Frontiers, they brought him to California to check the fit. There, they worked through the standards and even wrote a song together, 'Never Walk Away', which is included on *Revelation*. But Neal Schon abruptly ended the engagement with Hunsicker, telling him that it wouldn't work out.

Now comes the part of the story told so often it has become legend. In the movie *Don't Stop Believin': Every Man's Journey*, released in 2012, Schon tells how he scoured YouTube in desperation looking for a lead singer when he happened upon a talented young man in a cover band mimicking the style of many singers, including Steve Perry. The main challenge with this singer, Arnel Pineda, was his location. He lived in the Philippines.

After notifying Pineda that they were interested in bringing him in for an audition, he came to the United States and worked with the band for a few days. Each day, he improved, and after winning over Cain, he was offered the job. There are issues beyond the scope of this book about how Pineda was treated by some of the fans and even how his backstory is related by members of Journey. The movie, a documentary, does a commendable job of introducing Pineda to us and the challenges he faced, whether they were from his surroundings or caused by his own actions, and how he worked through them. He has a remarkable story.

For our purposes, though, the man can sing. To make *Revelation*, the band stayed at The Plant in Sausalito, and they brought back Kevin Shirley to produce. The outcome is a refreshing throwback to Journey's peak. *Revelation* is a natural evolution in the band's sound. Too often on *Arrival*, *Red 13* and *Generations*, Journey sounded like a different band or a band without a distinctive sound. They had good tracks here and there, but collectively, the albums were not very strong.

Revelation is a full truckload of content. One disc of original songs, though one is a new recording of 'Faith In The Heartland', another disc of new recordings of 11 Journey classics and a DVD of a show recorded at Planet Hollywood in Las Vegas together form a high-quality package that fans were craving at the time.

Working on their own label, Nomota ('no more tails', a swipe at Perry's preferred coat style while on stage), Journey signed an exclusive distribution agreement with Wal-Mart, by far the largest retailer in the United States. That deal worked out well for them. *Revelation* went Platinum, peaked on the *Billboard* chart at number five and spent 42 weeks on the chart. *Raised On Radio* was the last album to spend this long on the chart.

The large digipak has panels for nine works of art (including the front and back covers of the booklet). The art direction from Jeri Heiden features the work of Sarah Cumings. The front cover has an illustration, adapted from an illustration by Jason Dohanish, of the winged scarab rising above a red field surrounded by abstract flames. While each panel is different, they are similar in style, forming a cohesive package. The only quibble, and it's a minor one, is that the sky on the front and back covers is striped, looking like the Rising Sun symbol of the Japanese Empire of the early 20th century.

'Never Walk Away' (Schon, Cain, Jeremey Hunsicker) 4:16
This is a high-energy opener co-written by would-be lead vocalist Jeremey Hunsicker. Pineda pours it on, announcing that Journey have found their new voice. His work makes the song an enjoyable listen. The band are solid as

expected, keeping up the intensity through the four-minute run time. In the first verse, Pineda even tacks on an extra syllable to 'away', making it a Perry-esque 'away-ay'. But he is not a vocal clone; Pineda brings his own power and style to the mic.

With a catchy chorus – 'Will she run, or will she stay? Fool herself for one more day. Don't give up. Never walk away' – the song's subject seems to be the turmoil between Elizabeth and Jonathan Cain as they come to grips with the 'revelation' of his infidelities. Whatever the lyrical intent, the song deserves to be part of the Journey concert repertoire.

'Like A Sunshower' (Schon, Cain) 4:26
Schon and Cain must have decided that they needed the songs to emulate the 1980s version of Journey. This heir to 'Natural Thing' and 'Stay Awhile' is a fine change of pace from their usual balladeering. Opening with a simple guitar phrase before the beat sets in, Pineda nails the vocal. Throughout the tune, and especially during the chorus, the backing vocals shine. Cain's piano does the work that Rolie's Hammond B3 used to do, providing a musical surface for Schon to color the lyrics with some subtle guitar work. This is the kind of album track that would be sandwiched between the hits, making the listening experience of those Perry-Rolie albums such a pleasure.

'Change For The Better' (Schon, Cain) 5:49
The guitar begins this track with some crunchy stops before the band take over. Cain's signature is all over these lyrics about hitting a personal low and then deciding to do something about it. It's all uplifting and inspiring optimism. I don't mind optimism, but these power pop anthems feel like crowd-rousing music for a motivational speaker. Cain pens a number of these upbeat rockers, and I'd much rather listen to this than to cynical doom and gloom. Pineda's soaring rock vocals are superb. The chorus has that tight, on-the-beat, sing-along feel, but as a post-Perry track, it's only occasionally played live.

'Wildest Dream' (Schon, Cain) 4:59
This hard-rocking love song with an even higher tempo than 'Change For The Better' is a workout for all involved, including some strong, supportive synthesizer and piano work from Cain. Castronovo's relentless rhythm allows for the familiar Schon pyrotechnics, including a final jam that extends for over a minute to close it out. What the heck is this? Is it something from *Next*? Despite the speedy tempo and the cacophony of keys and frets, Journey seem loose and relaxed. They are enjoying themselves, and this is when they create something unexpected. Pineda's muscular vocals keep the effect in place as he improvises over the closing section. It isn't groundbreaking, but it is fun to hear Journey cut loose. This was one of the two songs ('After All These Years' is the other) from this album performed on the included live DVD.

'Faith In The Heartland' (Schon, Cain, Augeri) 6:15

The first of two re-recorded tracks from the Steve Augeri-era *Generations* album omits the extended keyboard intro, cutting the song by about 40 seconds. It helps, but it can't overcome the weaknesses of the original, even with Pineda's more emotive vocals. Maybe the mix is a little brighter and the instrumental separation is clearer, but the singsong-sewing-machine chorus is a lot to overcome. It's a competent track, but by no means is this overlong paean to the good people of middle America a classic, whether sung by Augeri or Pineda.

'After All These Years' (Cain) 4:07

The 15-second guitar and piano opening signals us to get those lighters out and start swaying because we have an incoming 'serious' ballad. As the first verse begins, Pineda comes close to imitating Dan Hill of 'Sometimes When We Touch' fame. Mercifully, Pineda picks up the momentum and performs the ballad, pausing when necessary to convey the right sincerity and then forcefully belting out the final chorus. It's all calculated, pretty and meant for radio.

However, when examining the lyrics of this song and the next two, we sense that we are in a three-song suite where Jonathan Cain is writing directly to his estranged wife, Liz. This first song is all about looking back on a long and fruitful relationship, tugging on the heartstrings of memories and shining the light on the good times. Cain lays out the argument for the value of what was and still could be, even though he might not have shown that he respected the relationship as much, considering his confessed infidelities while on tour. We will pick up this thread in the next track.

'After All These Years' performed well enough as a single to hit number nine on the *Billboard* Adult Contemporary chart, where it spent a respectable 26 weeks.

'Where Did I Lose Your Love' (Cain, Schon) 4:59

Opening with a power chord, dramatic keyboards and tumbling drums, this rocker maintains a steady pace but lacks melody. Pineda attempts to inject energy, imitating Perry a bit before the chorus. Schon's guitar phrases hint at Steve Lukather's work on 'Angela' from Toto's first album, yet fail to elevate the track. Castronovo's energetic rolls at the end are muted by uninspired keyboards. A potential 'Separate Ways'-inspired drum and keyboard moment fades out uninterestingly.

It's easy to see what Cain is up to on 'Where Did I Lose Your Love', the second of three songs that seem to be inspired by his failing marriage to Liz Cain. The track doesn't quite work as an admission of guilt or an apology. Cain regrets his infidelities and laments the relationship, but no lyrical confessions are forthcoming. This lack of contrition can perhaps be justified by a real sense of privacy and propriety to shield his family. Instead of a confession, we get this awkward rocker about how love should be eternal, but 'you left me'.

This track made it to number 19 on the *Adult Contemporary* chart, staying on for 20 weeks.

'What I Needed' (Schon, Cain) 5:25

The 15-second introduction of a piano melody doubled by the guitar announces a power ballad is on the way. The song doesn't seem as intentionally constructed for radio as 'After All These Years', yet it's a ballad that includes all the stirring emotion the band can muster. Pineda keeps some sorrow in his voice during the verses, which feature plenty of reverb. It sounds like Pineda harmonizing with himself on backing vocals during the syncopated chorus: 'You are ... what I needed'. The music wants to sound dramatic, but instead, it just sounds loud. The thundering drums, synthesized strings and bombastic guitar undercut a well-sung song of regret. The few sections where the music is quieter are much more effective.

This song is the final part of Cain's relationship triptych. Here, he acknowledges and accepts the loss and expresses his understanding that what he needed was right there, and he let it go. If 'After All These Years' is Cain asking for forgiveness in the name of the time spent building a family, and 'Where Did I Lose Your Love' an expression of 'woe is me' sorrow, then 'What I Needed' is saying that he will have to live with the consequences as he recognizes the thing he has lost. It's the most mature of the three. It's too bad it doesn't have more appropriate music to go with it.

'What It Takes to Win' (Cain, Schon) 5:25

Is this an 'Eye Of The Tiger' copy? Was this written for a sporting event? The song is about competing and winning. The words are adversarial, as if all competitions are zero-sum games with clear winners and losers. The verses are like inspirational nonsense written in a high school yearbook. I can appreciate the sentiment of rolling up the sleeves and putting in the hard hours to be successful, but I'd prefer to hear it explained in more original ways.

The track moves through the first verse with Pineda's gritty vocals. Schon's solo is quiet and uninspired. Despite aiming to be an anthem, it feels surprisingly subdued. Golland notes it sounds like a TV ad for a workout program or a Chevy pickup, which aptly describes its tame nature.

'Turn Down The World Tonight' (Cain) 4:58

Our second ballad with Cain as sole songwriter finds him continuing to explore his relationship stress. Here, the words sound more honest than 'After All These Years'. Pineda delivers a strong performance. Schon delivers one of his finer ballad solos, while Cain keeps the piano prominent and supportive throughout. It really is a fine song. This should have replaced either 'What I Needed' or 'Where Did I Lose Your Love' in Cain's earlier three-part relationship elegy.

'The Journey (Revelation)' (Schon) 5:25
This Schon instrumental would fit on most guitar virtuoso albums. Schon spins out original riffs, melodies and interesting progressions every day of his life. Given the track's slower tempo, it doesn't have that wow factor that many prefer in their instrumentals. 'The Journey (Revelation)' is a fine example of Schon's ability to create satisfying melodies and chord progressions.

The first half of the track is filled with exotic sounds from the keyboards and Pineda's eerie vocalese. Here, Schon stretches out and holds notes, building tension with a few well-placed runs. At the halfway point, Schon plays a phrase reminiscent of the opening to 'Lady Luck' (see *Evolution*). Castronovo and Valory join, and the song becomes a rock anthem for the next two minutes before the rhythm section vanishes. In the final minute of the song, Schon rapidly plays over a layer of keyboards and vocalese.

The track could have been shortened and served as an intro for the album, or they could have written some vocals over the middle section and carved that out as a song, or they could have chopped it up and done both. Here, though, we have five and a half minutes of Schon doing his thing, which, as of this writing, you can see on his social media clips every day. (See Schon's daily Instagram stories whenever Journey are not touring.)

Disc 2
This entire side is a re-recording of Journey's biggest hits with the current band lineup. For a deeper look at the songs, see the originals. Here, we will discuss differences and overall performances. The first thing that jumps out on this entire set is that the recording quality is so much better than the originals. Having said that, there is no doubt that the originals will always be the preferred versions. A couple of songs include an interesting change or two, so these are worth a closer listen.

'Only The Young' (Cain, Schon, Perry) 4:14
For this track, the song is practically identical to the original. Pineda mimics Perry's voice perfectly well. He is a talented singer.

'Don't Stop Believin'' (Cain, Schon, Perry) 4:55
Pineda doesn't extend vowel sounds quite like Perry, who makes words like 'feeling' or 'world' sound like they have additional syllables. It doesn't take away too much from the song; it's noticeable because we have heard the original so many times.

The band made a significant change in this re-recording. On *Escape*, 'Don't Stop Believin'' fades out, which they'd never performed this way in concert. Fans who've attended any shows or seen footage know that the song ends with everyone belting out 'Don't stop!' For the re-recorded version, the song goes on for 45 more seconds, tacking on another chorus repeat and adding that concert-style abrupt ending. No more fadeout. It's a good change and one that we are all familiar with from the live shows.

'Wheel In The Sky' (Schon, D. Valory, Fleischman) 5:01
About half the songs are slightly different from the originals, but a couple of them, like 'Wheel In The Sky', have some significant changes. The smallest change here is Cain's piano versus Rolie's Hammond B3. The second difference is that Gregg Rolie's unique vocals are not layered into the chorus. He added so much depth to Journey's backing vocals, and his absence turns a tremendous chorus into a merely adequate chorus. The third and largest change is the 45-second coda, where Castronovo provides a thunderous beat, Pineda sings 'round and round' over and over, and Schon lets rip with a stratospheric solo before the fade. This variation on the main melody brings the rock. I would have liked more variations like this from the originals, giving us an updated interpretation to enjoy. When the re-recordings sound like copies, we have no need to stray from the originals.

'Faithfully' (Cain) 4:47
If you're going to win over Jonathan Cain to be the singer in his band, you better be able to knock out this song and 'Open Arms' flawlessly, which does not mean mimicking Steve Perry. The former singer has a rounder tone, and the words flow out of him, while Pineda's tone is a bit sharper. When the singers hit these soaring choruses, Perry effortlessly hits the high notes, while Pineda relies more on powerfully belting out his lines. Pineda's voice gives these ballads more of a hard edge than Perry's. I like both, and it is an interesting exercise to compare the two singers. Meanwhile, Cain's piano sounds energetic, and perhaps because of the production quality, Schon's guitar playing has a more noticeable anthemic quality than the original.

'Any Way You Want It' (Schon, Perry) 3:25
Practically a note-for-note remake, this track is not as successful as the others. The band sound great; Pineda carries all the notes, and for a group of guys entering middle age, they bring the energy. But, like 'Wheel In The Sky' earlier, Rolie's spacious baritone is conspicuously absent. This has been a challenge for Journey when performing many of their songs before *Escape*, but most of us can easily ignore it. As studio remakes, though, Rolie's absence does detract from the experience.

'Who's Crying Now' (Cain, Perry) 5:16
'Who's Crying Now' is the least successful cover on the record. The vocal mix is tinny, and every element sounds like it was recorded at maximum volume. Valory's bass sounds sterile; his playing has no personality here. Listen to the early albums; the bass contribution, as Cain says in his memoir, sounds like a cello. The bass is such an important element of the opening of this song, and

here, it's lifeless. I praise the bass playing in the song's original entry. As I said there, this is an excellent composition, but here, Journey sound like a cover band.

'Separate Ways' (Cain, Perry) 5:27
Here is another nearly exact replica of the original, though with better sound.

'Lights' (Schon, Perry) 3:16
Of all the re-recordings, 'Lights', despite only being a few seconds longer, sounds the least like the original version. We've heard this on other Rolie-period covers. His voice is missed on those stacked harmonies. While Pineda's voice is expressive, it does not convey the longing for home heard in the original.

'Open Arms' (Cain, Perry) 3:22
This is Cain's second test for Pineda, and the singer delivers a ballad with vocal style differences as described in 'Faithfully' above. Pineda belts out the chorus, and you can hear him crank up the volume while Perry delivers smoother, more fluid crescendos. To give Pineda a break from the big ballads, lead vocals on 'Open Arms' were often given to Deen Castronovo on the *Revelation* tour. The recording quality shines through, with each instrument clear and balanced.

'Be Good To Yourself' (Schon, Cain, Perry) 4:29
The best track from *Raised On Radio* sounds stronger and cleaner here than the original. Pineda's voice comes closer to Perry's when singing the up-tempo rockers. We get to hear Ross Valory take on this excellent bass line, first performed by Randy Jackson, and he nails it. Schon's solo, in both versions, is among his best. He's given the final two minutes, about 30 seconds more than the original, to jam. His original one-and-a-half-minute solo was terrific, and here he is even better. The fadeout comes too quickly. This is one of the best covers on the album.

'Stone In Love' (Schon, Cain, Perry) 4:27
While this is an adequate remake, the track's famous guitar opening doesn't have the original's natural flow and energy. Schon sounds like a cover band guitarist over those first few bars, but he quickly returns to his normal self as the song continues. Pineda has proven that he can handle every song of the 'Dirty Dozen' he's asked to sing. (The band covered 11 of the 12, not re-recording 'Lovin' Touchin' Squeezin".)

Related Tracks
'Let It Take You Back' (Cain, Schon) 4:59
This is five minutes of nostalgia aimed at 50-year-old men that sounds like a cut from *Arrival*. The song threatens to rock, but its tired musical approach

never lifts off. Pineda pours himself into it, as do the band, but that can't make up for lackluster writing. Cain is normally a fine lyric writer, but his series of images, such as pool halls, record stores, Chevrolets and cigarettes, fail to amount to anything. Overall, this is a competent yet boring rock song. This track was available on the release of *Revelation* in Europe and Mexico.

'The Place In Your Heart' (Cain, Schon) 4:45
The band re-recorded their second track from *Generations,* and here they do change it up a little bit. The remake is nearly a half minute longer. Even though it is only one album later, the recording quality of *Revelation* is superior, with a brighter sound and clearer vocals. Schon's guitar solo has more power and is slightly longer. Cain's piano contributions are not hidden in *Generations'* muddy sound. 'The Place In Your Heart' was included on *Revelation*'s Japan release.

Eclipse (2011)

Personnel:
Jonathan Cain: keyboards, backing vocals
Deen Castronovo: drums, percussion, backing vocals
Arnel Pineda: lead vocals
Neal Schon: all guitars, backing vocals
Ross Valory: bass, backing vocals
Produce by Kevin Shirley, co-produced by Neal Schon and Jonathan Cain
Recorded at Fantasy Studios, Berkeley, California and The Blue Loft, County Q Nashville, Quad Nashville
Release date: 24 May 2011
Highest chart position: USA: 5; Platinum Certified
Running time: 1:06:20

After an intense level of touring, including a rare swing through Europe, Journey went back to the studio, this time returning to Fantasy Studios in Berkeley, where the magic happened with *Escape* and *Frontiers*. They had Kevin Shirley produce again. Later in the process, Shirley had competing commitments, so Schon and Cain gained co-producer credit as they worked to finish the final vocal and guitar overdubs.

With the success of *Revelation* and the last couple of years of touring, it was reasonable for Journey to keep creating new music. Other bands in the nostalgic 'heritage' market were also making new records. With Pineda out in front, they could record anything and keep the fans happy on tour with the original hits.

However, creative conflicts reared up at once. The two main songwriters, Schon and Cain, always brought their unique styles to each Journey record. Cain, comfortable penning heartfelt ballads, also wrote the lyrics for the harder-edged songs built from riffs and melodies brought by Schon. On *Eclipse*, Schon did not want any ballads. This could be seen as either bold, emphasizing the melodic rock side of Journey – or wrong-headed because the ballads tended to receive the most radio airplay and drove sales.

In the end, Schon won out. After *Eclipse*, it would be over a decade before Journey released a new album. That record, *Freedom*, had a radically different creative genesis, not only as a practical matter during the pandemic but also by the turmoil of creating *Eclipse*.

We're told that this is a concept album, but the concept is rather loosely about peace and spirituality. Tracks like 'City Of Hope', 'Chain Of Love', 'Tantra' and others touch on sacredness and express a generic spirituality. However, there is no overt message or story heard, as on many other bands' concept albums.

Jim Welch is back as the art director, and the cover features a brown monochromatic illustration by Gabor & Zoltan of the scarab, this time with axe-head wings blocking what we can assume to be a glowing orb. *Eclipse*, like *Escape* before it, is spelled with numbers: 'E-C-L-1-P-5-3'.

Repeating the approach to distribution and sales used for *Revelation*, this album was released exclusively via Wal-Mart and Journey's website. The album peaked at number 13 on the *Billboard* 200 album chart for one week in June 2011, shortly after its May release. It stayed on the charts for only five weeks, then briefly re-entered for two weeks in August, and that was it.

'City Of Hope' (Schon, Cain) 6:02
Schon sets the tone with a 30-second intro accompanied by drums. Pineda lends some gravitas to lyrics about staying optimistic in rough times. Despite this album focusing on Schon, the lyrics take a hard turn toward the spiritual and religious. Still, the song is intended as a singalong rock anthem, and for that purpose, it works. The last minute and a half of a six-minute track is an extended jam from Schon. It feels like a throwback to the days of *Look Into The Future* and *Next*. This 90-second section is a bit of a guitar indulgence, which might be an apt description of the entire album.
'City Of Hope' does receive a prominent place at the end of 2012's Arnel Pineda-focused documentary film *Don't Stop Believin': Every Man's Journey*.

'Edge Of The Moment' (Schon, Cain) 5:26
What happens when you take Cain's ballad lyrics and let Schon handle all the music? The answer is 'Edge Of The Moment'. Another unchanging, lengthy guitar opening is followed by Pineda delivering words in a traditional verse-verse-chorus-verse-chorus pattern. Throughout it all, Schon does his guitar hero schtick, never letting up.

'Chain Of Love' (Schon, Cain) 6:10
This is a throwback to the golden days of that pompous brand of 1980s heavy metal, sounding like a cross between Dio and Dokken. 'Chain Of Love', a song so unlike nearly all of Journey's catalog, is more enjoyable than it has any right to be. The track opens with a spacey 90 seconds of Cain imitating Jim Steinman on the piano. Pineda's lightly processed vocals help make this a blessed change of pace from the first two songs. Lyrically, we are inching ever closer to outright religiosity.
The track sounds like it belongs on a Whitesnake album, with its catchy hook and chorus. I can practically hear Don Dokken or David Coverdale singing this one. 'Chain Of Love' is one of my favorites on this album and of the post-Perry era.

'Tantra (My Eyes Can See)' (Schon, Cain) 6:27
Another epic-length (for Journey) track, this begins with a piano-driven intro section for the first 1:44. From this point, Schon takes on melodic duties, holding notes, giving it an anthemic feel. Pineda sings like he is Queensrÿche's Geoff Tate, with long, extended notes ending each verse.

'Tantra' does not have the catchy hook of 'Chain Of Love'. Lyrically, it is straight-up spirituality. With the word 'tantra' substituted for 'God', this feels like a tribute to the universal human need for meaning and how we can achieve that regardless of religion. I don't believe that Cain has suddenly become a spiritual universalist. This song is undoubtedly driven by his Christian faith, though it could easily be interpreted to be about Buddhism or The Force.

Pineda sings the following during the quiet, guitar-free coda, 'Across the universe the same force that moves the Earth's, in my heart, makes me whole, wash my doubt and fear away'. Sounds like the Jedi to me.

'Anything Is Possible' (Schon, Cain) 5:21
We have a fine four-minute pop-rock song that is stretched out beyond five minutes to allow Schon time to noodle on his guitar like this is 'Of A Lifetime'. The words are straight out of Journey's inspirational self-improvement hymnal: 'When you shoot for the moon and you miss your mark, baby, you'll still end up so high among the stars'. The song, to its credit, is never cloying despite the 'grab your dreams' sentiment.

In his memoir, Cain discusses his daughter's efforts to become a professional singer in Nashville, where Cain was building Addiction Studios. Madison's manager booked her an audition with a record company executive, only to have him treat her indifferently. Given this timing, it would be easy to interpret this as a father encouraging his daughter to keep at it. He's written about her before on *Generations* with 'Pride Of The Family'.

The track spent eight weeks on the *Billboard* Adult Contemporary chart, peaking at number 21. It was their last original hit on any of *Billboard*'s charts as of this writing.

'Resonate' (Schon, Cain) 5:11
After nearly a minute of ambient keyboard buildup, which does not add much, the song begins. Is it a love song? A hymn of praise masquerading as a love song? If this is Journey's version of the songs of Skillet, they could do far worse. Pineda's delivery is akin to Queensrÿche's Geoff Tate. Mercifully, Schon keeps the guitar antics under control, including a tight, convincing wrap-up instead of a sprawling jam. Although released as a single, this did not chart.

'She's A Mystery' (Schon, Cain, Pineda) 6:40
An unprecedented five of the 12 songs on *Eclipse* are over six minutes. In most cases, these tracks have worn out their welcome before completing, and while 'She's A Mystery' is not perfect, it's damn good. Schon plays acoustic, reminding us of Joe Satriani's work on 'Rubina's Blue Sky Happiness'. We're listening to Pineda sing a folk-tinged ballad, which he co-wrote with Cain and Schon. A string of metaphorical lines ending in 'she's a mystery' dominates

the verses. There's even a nod to Steve Augeri's 'Butterfly' in the verse: 'Like a gentle wind she moves. Her fascination I desire. She's a butterfly. She's a Mona Lisa smile'.

The bridge begins at the 3:40 mark, staying unruffled as if they were playing a laid-back version of the bridge from 'Stone In Love'. By this point, the song sounds like a cut from *Departure* or *Escape*.

Then, it all goes off the rails mere seconds before the five-minute mark. Schon revs up the guitar, and the song veers into clichéd Europop metal, with power chords seemingly cribbed from the likes of The Electric Boys. Pineda belts out a few more words, but this nearly two-minute ending is all about Schon soloing. He sounds fine, better than The Electric Boys, but it is an unnecessary addition to this fine track. The first five minutes of 'She's A Mystery' are a highlight here.

'Human Feel' (Schon, Cain) 6:43
Deen Castronovo delivers a tribal drum pattern reminiscent of REO Speedwagon's 'Don't Let Him Go'. Schon adds power chords that sound like Van Halen's 'Everybody Wants Some' but without the menace. Cain injects a little color with an organ-voiced synthesizer. 'Human Feel' could be interpreted as a metaphorical shaking fist when reaching a customer service line with an interactive voice response that never lets you reach a person. When we reach the 'Rise up' refrain, we might wonder how we got here from complaints about hardware and virtual worlds. It seems a bit of an overreaction, but it sounds like rock, and it makes for a good call and response in concert, though it was played rarely during the *Eclipse* tour. 'City Of Hope' and 'Edge Of The Moment' were far more likely to appear on the tour setlists.

This is the longest song on the record, yet it doesn't show its length until we reach another stretch of uninspired Schon guitar soloing. With no one to force his hand, he does what he thinks is best, which is playing spontaneously. His solos on the classics have a strong relationship to the song's melody. On most of the *Eclipse* tracks, we hear a decent song, such as this one, suddenly forced to make way for Schon to cut loose. Sometimes, that works, but more often, it simply extends the song and reduces its power. There is a way to inject solos into these tracks. Schon has done this many times before with incredible skill and musicality. The skill is there, but here he is adrift.

'Ritual' (Schon, Cain) 4:56
Journey pull off a power-pop rock song without a 90-second guitar solo. That alone separates this from most of the album. 'Ritual' has some fleeting moments that remind us of Journey in 1980. For example, around the 50-second mark, as the first chorus is about to begin, the guitar and piano set up Pineda's vocals. It's a little thing that Journey mostly abandoned from *Raised On Radio* onward.

'Ritual' fits the post-Perry songwriting approach and is part of a family that includes songs such as 'Never Walk Away', 'Higher Place' and 'I Got A Reason'. All these tunes have catchy hooks and choruses that concert crowds love, but they don't have that special Journey touch, which we argued earlier is caused by a lack of Steve Perry in the songwriting process.

'To Whom It May Concern' (Pineda, Schon, Cain, Erik Pineda) 5:15
If Journey wanted to exploit the Contemporary Christian Music market, they would be kings of the Christian rock hill. While these lyrics are not overtly Christian, the veil is thin and easy to see through. 'To Whom It May Concern' could be mistaken for a song by Petra or Third Day, with Tommy Shaw as the guest lead singer. For the best example of Pineda sounding like the Styx and Damn Yankees singer, listen around the 3:20 mark, including his vocalizing over parts of Schon's solo (around 4:06).

Cain's synthesizers and piano make a welcome appearance and not merely as textural additions. The song plods a bit and somehow manages to sound like a downer despite its hopeful message and wish for a better world. These lyrics tread well-worn, albeit well-meant, ground. Written by, we assume, Cain and the two Pinedas (no relation to each other), the words lack punch, which is a shame.

'Someone' (Schon, Cain) 4:34
In so many ways, 'Someone' is a throwback to the album-filling tracks of pop-rock Journey. It isn't single material, but I don't complain when the song comes up in the queue. Pineda's lead and the backing vocals are strong and clear. Schon's guitar work is solid, with a satisfying solo to play out the song. The lyrics, well-trod ground about finding love when you're feeling lonely, touch all the bases, from wasting time at bars until the last call to acknowledging that everyone has had tough relationships. 'Someone' feels like an optimistic scolding. It's Journey having a little fun.

'Venus' (Schon) 3:34
I hate to send you back to 'To Whom It May Concern', but it's necessary to understand this instrumental track. Around the 4:18 mark of the earlier song, Schon begins playing a minute-long, uplifting guitar melody in yet another instrumental coda.

On 'Venus', after the intro, Schon continues that same melody over drums and bass, though, this time, he throws in some minor chords here and there. About half a minute in, his furious, overdubbed solo takes the spotlight. This continues for a couple of minutes before another fadeout, and then it returns one final time. It's as if we were back in 1974.

Why not include this as a second part of 'To Whom It May Concern'? Why insert 'Someone' between these tracks? Maybe 'Someone' and 'Ritual' are too musically alike to be back-to-back. They had a potential epic here – given the guitar indulgences on many of the other album tracks, it wouldn't have been too much for *Eclipse* to have a nine-minute song.

Solo Work, Relationships, Arrests And The Hall Of Fame (2011-2019)

The story of Journey during the 2010s is that of a hard-touring heritage band crisscrossing the United States, heading to Europe and making their first trip through Australia and New Zealand. These years were also musically creative times for side projects and solo efforts by everyone in the band.

Schon, Cain and Arnel Pineda released one or more solo albums between the release of *Eclipse* and *Live In Japan 2017*. Pineda's release, *AP*, was independently done in 2015, as was his EP of four Christmas songs, *Sounds Of Christmas*, that same year.

Cain and Liz ended up filing for divorce and they separated. During this time, the band, who had not yet returned to using private jets, had to fly on Southwest Airlines because of some business Cain had to attend to for his winery. According to his memoirs, he found himself sitting across the aisle from Paula White. She is a pastor of the so-called prosperity gospel of popular Christianity, known for its megachurches and televangelism. Cain's burgeoning religiosity went into overdrive. He and White married, and Cain began recording Christian music, releasing *What God Wants To Hear* in 2016 and his own Christmas album, *Unsung Noel*, in 2017.

Cain's marriage to White also brought with it her relationship with the Trump Administration. She delivered a prayer at his inauguration. Later, they were invited to the White House. Cain asked Ross Valory and Arnel Pineda to attend, and they did. Schon was livid, not because he was not invited, but because he wanted Journey to have no political affiliation. There was no need to alienate any fans over politics. Journey played at the Republican National Convention in 2016, but Schon viewed it as a commercial rather than a political transaction. Journey had not donated their time; they were well paid. When the 2020 GOP Convention came calling, Journey declined.

Schon, who never stops playing, released several solo albums, including reuniting with Steve Smith and Jan Hammer for *The Calling* in 2012. He teamed up with bassist Marco Mendoza, who we will meet again shortly, and Deen Castronovo to make 2014's *So U*. In 2015, Schon played guitar and bass on his double album *Vortex*. Smith was, once again, on drums and Igor Len on keyboards. Schon wrote all the songs alone or with Smith or Len. Cain joined him for one song, 'Triumph Of Love'.

Perhaps the biggest sensation during this period was the reunion of most of the remaining members of the original Santana lineup, including Schon and Gregg Rolie, for the release of *Santana IV* in 2016. Yet, the album, released on the Santana IV label (Santana were with RCA in 2016), didn't produce any hits. To capture this historic reunion, a two-and-a-half-hour, triple-live album, *Santana IV Live At The House Of Blues Las Vegas*, came out the same year on the Eagle Vision label.

The biggest change in Schon's life was his marriage to Michaele Salahi. I'll not provide the details, salacious or otherwise, of the story of how they wound up together. Shortly after her divorce, Schon proposed to her on stage during a concert, presenting her with a gaudy diamond. The Pay-Per-View wedding included a performance by Journey. She's been a constant presence by Schon's side and his side of the stage during performances since the *Eclipse* days.

With Deen Castronovo's singing being used more by Journey during live shows, people took notice, including Serafino Perugino of Italy's Frontiers Records. The keeper of the melodic rock flame throughout the world, Perugino built a band, Revolution Saints, with Castronovo as the vocal centerpiece. Their first album, *Revolution Saints*, was released in 2015, with Jack Blades on bass, Doug Aldrich on guitar and singer-composer-keyboardist Alessandro Del Vecchio. In 2017, they released *Light In The Dark*.

Castronovo, however busy he was during this time, was battling addiction. After an arrest for endangering and harassing his girlfriend in 2012, in the summer of 2015, he attacked and sexually assaulted her. He was high when arrested. By that fall, he had pleaded guilty to domestic abuse and received treatment while on probation. While Castronovo was working to get his life back from the depths of addiction and violence, Journey needed to find a drummer.

Steve Smith was a busy man, too, leading his jazz ensemble Vital Information and serving as an ambassador for drumming around the country. He was a fixture on the pages of *Modern Drummer*. Smith was really the only formally trained musician Journey ever had. When he worked on *The Calling* and *Vortex*, Schon was surprised that Smith wrote out the drum parts. Smith was offered the job, but he had other commitments. Journey hired drummer Omar Hakim to cover the touring while Smith kept those commitments. Once he was available, he rejoined Journey. (To be clear, Smith was and had been a partner of Nightmare Productions, which is the corporate entity that owns Journey, but we are talking about performing, not the business.)

In April 2017, Journey were inducted into the Rock & Roll Hall of Fame in a class that included the Electric Light Orchestra, Pearl Jam, Yes, Joan Baez and, posthumously, Tupac Shakur. (Nile Rodgers was inducted for musical excellence, too.) Inductees from Journey included Schon, Cain, Smith and Valory from the 2017 lineup, as well as former band members Aynsley Dunbar, Gregg Rolie, and, of course, Steve Perry. This was Rolie's second ceremony; he was inducted with his Santana bandmates in 1998. Each band member spoke, expressing gratitude toward the fans, other band members and even Herbie Herbert, who was in the audience. Steve Perry went out of his way to single out Herbie for bringing him into the band.

Traditionally, inductees perform a few songs from their catalog, so anticipation grew around the possibility that Perry would finally sing with Journey again. It was not to be. Luckily, Pineda was there to provide the vocals.

Freedom (2022)

Personnel:
Jonathan Cain: piano, keyboards, vocals
Deen Castronovo: lead vocals on 'After Glow'
Jason Derlatka: background vocals
Randy Jackson: bass, background vocals
Arnel Pineda: lead vocals
Neal Schon: lead guitar, keyboards, vocals
Narada Michael Walden: drums, keyboards, background vocals
Co-produced by Narada Michael Walden and Neal Schon
Arranged by Neal Schon
Recorded at Tarpan Studios, San Rafael, California
Additional studios: Dreamsong, Orlando, Florida; Addiction Sound, Nashville, Tennessee; Yo Mama's House & L.A. NRG Studios, North Hollywood, California; Left on Sunset, Hollywood, California
Release Date: 8 July 2022
Highest Chart Position: US: 88
Running Time: 1:13:12

As we make our way through the most recent years, Journey's history is marked by seemingly constant litigation as suits and countersuits are filed for serious business issues and silly personal squabbles. A cynic would say that these noisy lawsuits could be part of a plan to stay in the news. A band make news by touring and composing music. Neal Schon loves doing both activities, but he also has a litigious side and, evidently, a sizeable ego. Journey have made a lot of money over the years, and with private jets, expensive Italian sports cars, 13-plus-carat diamonds, roses filling heated swimming pools in the northern California hills and a guitar collection worthy of the Smithsonian, one could say that, while Schon enjoys the spoils, he likes it when it's noticed.

Schon has come to think of himself as the owner and caretaker of Journey. Given his actions in creating another act called Neal Schon's Journey Through Time and the creation of Schon Productions, a few of the band members looked to level out the playing field for management of Nightmare, the entity that owns Journey. After a by-the-book election of new officers, including Steve Smith and Ross Valory, Schon tried to fire them, his long-time business partners, from the band. He tried this through manager John Baruck, and when he refused, Schon fired him and Azoff Management. Once all the legal dust settled with suits and countersuits, Smith and Valory were out as performers in Journey, though they are still partners in Nightmare. This left Cain and Schon as the only two owners who still performed as Journey. They became the band's co-managers. If you're interested in a detailed blow-by-blow of all this legal maneuvering, check out Golland (see bibliography).

Irrational squabbles led to more court filings and acrimony, but the lure of continued paydays kept the 'marriage', as Cain metaphorically refers to their relationship, together. Schon would test the limits of that relationship and others with his effort to market *Journey Through Time* in 2023, even planning some shows. We will look closer at that release shortly.

With COVID-19 appearing in early 2020 and lockdowns in place, touring was not an option. Schon, like a shark that can't stop swimming, needed to create. To replace Smith and Valory, Schon turned to some old friends. On bass, Randy Jackson, by now a household name in the United States for his work as a judge on *American Idol*, returned to Journey after having played bass on *Raised On Radio* and the following tour back in 1986-87. (He also played bass on *Frontiers*' 'After The Fall'.)

For drums, Schon turned to former Mahavishnu Orchestra drummer, multi-instrumentalist, composer, and producer Narada Michael Walden, who also had hit solo records in the 1970s and 1980s. Walden, as a producer, has worked with many artists over the years, including recently teaming with Schon for his solo album, *Universe* (2020). Walden, the songwriter, has credits on 13 of 15 tracks on *Freedom*.

Schon decided that the album title for this new version of Journey would be *Freedom*, the intended title for *Raised On Radio*. It's a nod to the old days and an acknowledgement of the impact of COVID-19 on the world. Journey released the first song from *Freedom* – 'The Way We Used To Be', a song about how our lives were affected by the pandemic – in the summer of 2021 as a preview of the album. It's a good example of what to expect from this new iteration of Journey: competent performances, interesting drumming from Walden, generic lyrics and some rough choruses.

Work on the album continued, with six studios used as part of the recording process, allowing the band members to work in their own spaces. Pineda recorded vocals from the Philippines on his laptop, with Walden and engineer Jim Reitzel connecting from California. The laborious process worked, though the seams show here and there, as we will hear. Jason Derlatka makes his first appearance on a Journey album, having recently toured with them as the added keyboardist and backing vocalist.

Jim Welch continues his work as art director for the album packaging. The scarab logos on the front and back covers are classic designs. The back cover planet has the encircling torus harking back to the earlier albums. These designs look digitally created, as they undoubtedly are, which makes old fans like me wistful of the days of paintings and pen and ink creations. They can feel just a few steps above clipart.

Individual band photos are limited to Cain, Schon and Pineda. Walden's only photo appearance in the album package is with Schon. The pamphlet features a highly saturated photo of the iconic West and East Mitten Buttes in Monument Valley, Arizona. The photo was taken around one of the equinoxes when one butte casts a shadow on the other. The sky is a stylized time-lapse of an orb moving across the panorama amid rays of star streaks.

'Together We Run' (Walden, Rachel Efron, Jackson, Cain, Schon) 4:49
Oakland-based jazz singer, songwriter and pianist Rachel Efron, who has since written a song ('So Beautiful') for Walden's 2023 solo album *Euphoria*, wrote 'Together We Run', with the full band (except Pineda) receiving co-writing credit. Like many a Journey song, the piano begins with a minor key melody, showing that serious subject matter awaits. Cain and Walden supply keyboards with synthesized strings under Pineda's vocals. By the time Walden's drums and Jackson's bass announce the arrival of the chorus, we know we are in one of Journey's uplifting songs.

Pineda sings, 'Together we run straight to the city lights. Together we run, our lives begin tonight', while, simultaneously, Jackson sings, 'Don't give up or you'll lose the fight' and 'Hold on to this with all your might', before the unfortunate 'whoa, whoa, whoa' line kicks in. Exactly what is the subject matter of this song? Is it about a misunderstood musician trying to make it in the big city? With the opening verses, they pull back into the safe realm of innocuous cheerleading for a generic underdog.

Walden brings plenty of energy to the percussion, sounding confident. Schon somehow keeps himself in check for the first three minutes before delivering a short bridge solo. He finally cuts loose in classic fashion at the 4:12 mark. He sounds great, but we only have a few seconds left of the song. A bit more of Walden's drumming and a bit less of that awful 'whoa, whoa' line in the chorus would make this more listenable.

'Don't Give Up On Us' (Schon, Cain, Walden) 5:23
Your ears are not playing tricks on you; that intro you hear does sound a lot like 'Separate Ways (Worlds Apart)', with its solo synthesizer opening joined by a rumbling rhythm section. The similarities quickly fade as the song drifts into bland Cain lyric territory about failing love and mutual blame: 'Just know we can't quit now'. The words 'walk away' appear in the chorus, continuing a practice for post-Perry Journey albums.

The chorus sounds like a pop version of the verses in Ted Nugent's 'Stranglehold', but there's no raw emotion here, only the Hallmark sentimentality that plagues many post-Perry era ballads. Schon, once again, saves his guitar until the second half of the song, but, again, it is too little, too late.

'Don't Give Up On Us', like much of this album, suffers from a muddy sound. Maybe it was the quality of Pineda's laptop.

Released as a single, this did not chart.

'Still Believe In Love' (Schon, Cain, Walden) 5:16
Journey border on sounding like a boy band with their vocal harmonies, this time with a spacey, sophisticated r&b feel. This is Adult Contemporary gold,

but they didn't release it as a single. Everybody sings backing vocals, including Jason Derlatka, making his first appearance with Journey on record. Jackson doesn't perform on this song, with Cain playing synth bass. Schon adds some work on the keyboards, too.

Schon's guitar work elevates this song slightly above the usual ho-hum boredom of these interchangeable love songs.

'You Got The Best Of Me' (Schon, Cain, Walden) 5:33
The never-ending 'You got it, you want it, you got the best of me' wears out its welcome long before the five and half minutes have passed. Moreover, the end of the second verse has the following words: 'Never walk away'.

Schon, again, has a small keyboard part. Based on the awkward synthesizer intro, this is likely his handiwork. Schon's guitar opening reminds me of Eddie Van Halen's guitar coda on *Diver Down*'s 'Little Guitars'. At the end of 'You Got The Best Of Me', Schon repeats the guitar part – the likeness to 'Little Guitars' is undeniable.

Jackson is back on bass, and he and Walden provide a great foundation for what should be a signature Journey song. That repeated chorus is a lot to absorb as it dominates the track.

This was released as a single but did not chart – a missed opportunity.

'Live To Love Again' (Cain) 5:30
A solo Cain writing credit means that we are at the 'Faithfully' remake track. He does not disappoint, writing a power ballad that leaves nothing on the table. Pineda is up to the task, and Schon performs his power ballad guitar solo magic once again. Will this take the place of 'Open Arms' or 'Faithfully' or rise above their other copycat versions of these two classics? No, but that doesn't mean they've crafted a bad song. This is fine, and in that alternate timeline where Journey focus on their Adult Contemporary chops, this is a megahit that they would include in their show on the Las Vegas Strip.

'The Way We Used to Be' (Schon, Cain) 3:35
Albums made between 2020 and 2022 are going to have a track that acknowledges the impact of COVID-19. Instead of dealing with death or controversy, 'The Way We Used To Be' laments the lack of human contact and the uncertainty plaguing everyone. Schon and Cain put together a solid rock song that the band deliver with easy competence. This is a track where I would have welcomed another 30 seconds of Schon tearing up the frets; fading out just as Schon heats up is such a downer.

'Come Away With Me' (Schon, Cain, Walden) 4:02
A throwback to the 1970s, this sounds like something from the pre-Perry days. You expect to hear Rolie's Hammond B3 and his distinctive vocals, but instead, we have Walden pounding out the rhythm and Jackson showing off

his bass skills. That is more than enough to provide a foundation for Schon's riffing and an excellent rock vocal from Pineda. The sound isn't perfect by any means, but the muddy mix fits this song well. They sound like a talented young band performing at a bar on a Friday night. This is a band approaching their 50th year of existence, so sit back and let them play. This is one of the best songs on the record.

'After Glow' (Schon, Cain, Walden) 5:22
Deen Castronovo was let go from the band for his domestic violence arrest and conviction. As he set about reforming his ways and getting his life back, his former bandmates had work for him. Cain had him play on his first Christian solo album, *What God Wants To Hear*, in 2016, and Schon hired him to play drums with the short-lived side project Journey Through Time. Castronovo's appearance on *Freedom* is for this single track, and he serves as lead vocalist, not the drummer. However, during the summer of 2021, as we will see in the Lollapalooza performance, Castronovo is back on the drum throne, where he is, as of this writing, Journey's drummer once again.

The song is a serious misfire, though, and it has nothing to do with Castronovo's vocal abilities. Trying to tread similar ground as 'Still Believe In Love', it falls apart with problematic backing vocals and a terrible chorus. Even Schon's fiery attempts to save it fall short. Every band has a few embarrassing moments, and here we have one of Journey's biggest. While Walden's drumming has been between good and incredible for most of the album, he gets carried away with himself at times, like Marty McFly on guitar at the high school dance in *Back To The Future*. He teetered on the edge in 'Together We Run', and here he takes the leap. The drums are all over the place in the latter moments of the song. Maybe drummers will love it, but it makes me feel a bit overwhelmed.

'Let It Rain' (Schon, Cain, Walden) 4:40
As if to make up for the misstep of 'After Glow', Journey return to their bluesy, hard rock best with 'Let It Rain'. Schon opens it up with a sturdy guitar riff, and Walden and Jackson join to turn this into a lurching 1970s metal groove. Cain's keyboards provide the cushion for all this thunder, and Pineda channels some Montrose-era Sammy Hagar.

Like 'Come Away With Me', this is not the usual Journey hard rocker. This harkens back to the early days and, for me, it is a welcome change. More of this reinvention is necessary if they are going to keep creating new music.

This was released as a single but did not chart.

'Holdin' On' (Schon, Cain, Jackson, Walden) 3:14
'Holdin' On' is tight, efficient hard rock that suffers from the sound quality issues that plague the album. Schon, in his element here, tears through his parts with his finely honed skills. In his late 60s, he sounds as dexterous and

fast as any 25-year-old. Also, throughout the album, Jackson's bass has been mostly unaffected, driving the music through the muddy mix. Unfortunately, on this track, Pineda sounds like he's singing through a traffic cone – the song deserves a better sound. This harder version of Journey is fun; it's too bad these songs won't make the lucrative 'heritage' circuit setlists.

'All Day And All Night' (Schon, Cain, Walden) 3:38

Another short, groove-laden blues rock song has me wondering if we've wandered onto a totally different playlist. If Journey put out an entire album of these songs, I wouldn't complain.

Though Cain is a co-writer here, he did not perform on this track. Walden provides the keyboards. The sound quality is a little better. The bad sound tends to show up when the song crescendos, clipping Pineda's vocals and giving everything a foggy feel.

The song could not be simpler, with direct verses about love and desire. Digging deep into the hair metal catalog, I found this reminiscent of the debut album by The Bullet Boys, which is not a bad thing. Journey are having fun.

'Don't Go' (Pineda, Schon, Walden, Cain) 4:58

Pineda joins the songwriting team on this standard, chorus-repeating pop song. It's great to hear the rare song on *Freedom* that is in a major key – the bright, bouncy optimism sets it apart from the rest of the record. The chorus – 'Don't go. Oh, baby, don't go. Don't go. I need you darling' – is repeated enough to take up nearly half the song's running time. Catchy choruses can earn that sort of space. 'Don't Go' does not have that quality and it becomes a slog to listen to by the bridge. Schon's solo fits the song but doesn't have that magic, either. Cain, though a co-writer, does not perform on this track. This time, the few keyboard needs are supplied by Schon.

'United We Stand' (Schon, Cain, Walden, Jackson) 5:05

This track sounds mostly like classic Journey. Pineda's vocals are top-shelf on 'United We Stand'. When the chorus rolls around, Pineda soars with 'United we stand, divided we fall' but the backing vocals add a breathy 'united' or 'divided' ahead of each respective line. To me, it sounds out of place and lessens the chorus' power.

'United We Stand' is a relationship song in the Cain mold. The lyrics restate a generic 'I'm better with you than without you' message. Here, the chorus takes on added meaning in a world of COVID-19 lockdowns, wars and a divisive political climate. It's better to be in love in the bad times than not. Deservedly released as a single, this did not chart.

'Life Rolls On' (Schon, Walden) 4:57

The first minute and 45 seconds remind me of 'Liberty', and for a moment, we have the sense that Steve Perry has returned to co-write a song. These nostalgic lyrics look to the past with gratitude while being optimistic about the future. Pineda sings these with the right touch of weary wisdom.

After this two-minute opening, Schon fires up the six-string. When Walden and Jackson thunder in, Pineda sings with gusto about that optimistic future. With nearly two minutes to go, Schon delivers an extended solo with Pineda repeating 'Life rolls on' atop the fireworks, which takes us to the end of this solid track.

'Beautiful As You Are' (Schon, Cain, Walden) 7:10
Schon is aching to take the band full circle, reliving the wide-open compositions of the early days. One of the longest tracks in Journey's studio output opens with Schon's acoustic guitar playing a quiet melody over a bed of synthesized strings. Pineda has a chance to show a little range. He shows his charm, if not his confidence. This first section lasts shy of 90 seconds and serves as an extended introduction to the main song.

Electric guitar, bass and drums pick up the pace with a classic sequence that somehow sounds tentative. Yet, this is in their wheelhouse, and with a thumping rhythm section and the guitar building tension, this begins to sound like a cut from *Escape*. Like other tracks on this record, the backing vocals drone on without charm during the chorus. So much of this album's music is a refreshing throwback to the early days, but the mix and the lackluster choruses undermine its strengths.

Toward the end of this main section, Schon delivers his solo, threatening to overheat but keeping it in check. Walden has some fine moments here, too, seeming to know this is the last track (at least on the non-Japanese releases). His drums are assertive and musical and help heighten the tension before a coda that returns to the quiet acoustic of the intro.

Lyrically, this feels like Cain singing to his wife, Paula White. Or maybe it's Schon writing to his beloved Lady M. Either way, it serves the purpose of expressing love, gratitude and respect for a life partner. We must give Walden credit for bringing out better compositions from his two writing partners than those on *Eclipse*.

Related Track
'Hard To Let It Go' (Cain) 4:08
The last studio track is this classic Cain piano ballad that was included as a bonus track on the Japan release of *Freedom*. It's a gorgeous entry in Journey's post-Perry Adult Contemporary playlist. Schon delivers a simple, effective solo. Pineda does his best crooning on the record, and the backing vocals do not detract from the overall impression.

The song is also a part of the COVID-19 song catalog, lamenting the lack of live performances and the adoration of the crowds. There are a few tendentious lines, bordering on political, that stay inside the boundaries that would otherwise upset this band's fragile balance: 'Freedoms they try to take from you. All this world's going through. They can't take away what I was born to do'. Cain, however, keeps it about perseverance instead of persecution. The song is a fine reflection of the times, and it sounds good. If you can find it, this is worth a listen.

Compilations

In The Beginning (1979)
Re-mastered and sequenced by Kevin Elson
Release date: November 1979
Highest chart position: US: 152
Tracklisting: 'Of A Lifetime', 'Topaz', 'Kohoutek', 'On A Saturday Nite', 'It's All Too Much', 'In My Lonely Feeling/Conversations', 'Mystery Mountain', 'Spaceman', 'People', 'Anyway', 'You're On Your Own', 'Look Into The Future', 'Nickel & Dime', 'I'm Gonna Leave You'

Not one to leave cash on the table, Herbie Herbert took advantage of Journey's burgeoning popularity by releasing this double album in late 1979 – between the releases of *Evolution* and *Departure*. It serves as a 'best of' the first three pre-Perry albums: *Journey*, *Look Into The Future* and *Next*.

There is a possibility that this release backfired on the band. Curious fans bought it and were a bit confused since it sounded nothing like the Journey they were hearing on the radio. It hit the charts in January and was gone by February. It debuted on the charts in January 1980, peaked in February, and by the time of the release of *Departure*, fans had moved on.

In The Beginning never had a CD release, but one can find vinyl copies. The gatefold cover features artwork by Mouse, with a black planet in the center of the Journey wing motif, all orbited by the word 'Journey'. Herbie wanted customers to know they were seeing a Journey album when perusing the stores – this one was tough to miss. 'Journey' and the album title are at the top of the cover, while the years '1975-1977' are at the bottom. Inside the gatefold is a simple wordless illustration, again by Mouse, of a series of black orbs that are either rising or descending in a desert with a sun either rising or sitting behind the distant mountains on the horizon.

While collectors will seek this album, even if only to display the cover, for those only interested in the music, you are better served by owning or streaming the first three albums in their entirety.

Greatest Hits (1988)
Production coordination: Kevin Elson
Release date: 15 November 1988
Highest chart position: US: 10, Diamond Certified (18x Platinum)
Tracklisting: 'Only The Young', 'Don't Stop Believin'', 'Wheel In The Sky', 'Faithfully', 'I'll Be Alright Without You', 'Any Way You Want It', 'Ask The Lonely', 'Who's Crying Now', 'Separate Ways (Worlds Apart)', 'Lights', 'Lovin', Touchin', Squeezin'', 'Open Arms', 'Girl Can't Help It', 'Send Her My Love', 'Be Good To Yourself', 'When You Love A Woman'

The original *Greatest Hits* album was released while the band were on hiatus and is one of the most successful albums ever in the United States. After its original release, it first hit the chart in December 1988, peaking at number ten on 11 February 1989 and staying on the chart for 92 weeks, exiting in late

October 1991. With the resurgence in Journey's popularity in the late 2000s caused by 'Don't Stop Believin'' appearing everywhere and the success of *Revelation,* 'Greatest Hits' reentered the chart on 5 December 2009 and, as of this writing, is still there. By the spring of 2024, the album will reach the milestone of 800 weeks on the chart.

Only two albums have longer chart histories on the *Billboard* Hot 200 than Journey's *Greatest Hits*: Pink Floyd's *Dark Side Of The Moon* and *Legend – The Best Of Bob Marley & The Wailers.* It's difficult to overstate the enormity and longevity of this type of success. As of early 2024, these are the only three albums with over 750 weeks on the chart. *Billboard* changed the rules for older albums, making it even more difficult to stay on the main 200 chart. They've created a Catalog Albums Top 50 to move any of these titles that fall out of the top 100 of the Hot 200.

The 2006 CD release added one track from *Trial By Fire.* The album cover features a Kelley illustration of the winged scarab vertically centered between red and blue orbs, sticking with the traditional Journey motif. Gracing the back cover is a stylistic photo of the band, each wearing headphones and gathered around a boom to record some vocals. A black and white full-body band photo graces the inner sleeve.

The Ballade (1991)

Release date: 12 December 1991 (Japan)
Tracklisting: 'Open Arms', 'Lights', 'Too Late', 'Faithfully', 'I'll Be Alright Without You', 'Patiently', 'Who's Crying Now', 'After The Fall', 'The Eyes Of A Woman', 'Opened The Door', 'Good Morning Girl', 'Stay Awhile', 'Still They Ride', 'Send Her My Love', 'Why Can't This Night Go On Forever'
The 15 tracks collected here are from *Infinity* through *Raised On Radio.* Only ballads and soft love songs make the cut. No guitar-driven rock is on this record. This Japan-only release has a distinctive cover. Within a black border is an illustration of an ancient wall of rock 'n' roll hieroglyphs, such as a treble clef, notes, guitars, drums and cymbals. Among the pictograms are the letters 'JRNY' and a lavender scarab crawls on the wall. While this is of interest to collectors, others who want physical media of the hits will find all these tracks, except 'Opened The Door' from *Infinity*, on other compilations.

Time^3 (1992)

Producer: Don DeVita
Liner notes: Joel Selvin, updated by Dan Pine
Art direction: Jim Welch
Cover art: Stanley Mouse
Release date: 12 December 1992
Highest chart position: US: 90; Gold Certified
Running time: 3:50:39
Tracklisting:

Time1: 'Of A Lifetime', 'Kohoutek', 'I'm Gonna Leave You', 'Cookie Duster', 'Nickel & Dime', 'For You', 'Velvet Curtain/Feeling That Way', 'Anytime', 'Patiently', 'Good Times', 'Majestic', 'Too Late', 'Sweet And Simple', 'Just The Same Way', 'Little Girl', 'Any Way You Want It', 'Someday Soon', 'Good Morning Girl'

Time2: 'Where Were You', 'Line Of Fire', 'Homemade Love', 'Natural Thing', 'Lights (Live)', Stay Awhile (Live)', 'Walks Like A Lady (Live)', 'Lovin', Touchin', Squeezin' (Live)', 'Dixie Highway (Live)', 'Wheel In The Sky (Live)', 'Don't Stop Believin'', 'Stone In Love', 'Keep On Runnin'', 'Who's Cryin' Now', 'Still They Ride', 'Open Arms', 'Mother, Father'

Time3: 'La Raza Del Sol (Alternate Version)', 'Only Solutions', 'Liberty', 'Separate Ways (Worlds Apart)', 'Send Her My Love', 'Faithfully', 'After The Fall', 'All That Really Matters', 'The Eyes Of A Woman', 'Why Can't This Night Go On Forever', 'Once You Love Somebody', 'Happy To Give', 'Be Good To Yourself', 'Only The Young', 'Ask The Lonely', 'With A Tear', 'Into Your Arms', 'Girl Can't Help It (Live Video Mix)', 'I'll Be Alright Without You (Live Video Mix)'

By the end of 1992, Journey band members were working in various combinations in bands like The Storm, Bad English and Hardline. Steve Smith kept busy with his jazz ensemble, Vital Information. Journey's *Greatest Hits* had come and gone from the charts. Fans were ready for the band to reform and record. That, however, was years away. Knowing the demand was there and not willing to put out another repackaging of the same dozen or so hits, Columbia Records did what many labels have done with an artist's extensive catalog: they compiled a box set.

The best box sets present a comprehensive overview of the band's output, including minor hits, concert favorites and critical deep cuts, and they throw in unreleased tracks, alternate takes and demos, rare live recordings and studio experiments. *Time^3*, pronounced 'Time Cubed', is all this and more. The marvelous liner notes by Joel Selvin, the plethora of photos, and the outstanding track descriptions were the best remedy for those of us suffering from the lack of new Journey music. Arranged chronologically, the tracks listed above are covered in detail with their proper albums or in the album's 'Related Tracks' section.

Like many box sets, it was expensive, but it generated enough sales to break into the *Billboard* album chart for a few weeks. The artwork by Mouse features the scarab diving into a planet's lava-crusted surface, symbolizing that we are going deep into the catalog instead of heading off to new places. *Time^3* is a must-have for hardcore Journey fans, and it is available on most popular streaming services.

Two songs charted from this set. 'Natural Thing' spent five weeks on the Mainstream Rock Airplay chart, peaking at number 32, while the live version of 'Lights' was on the Adult Contemporary chart for ten weeks, peaking at number 30.

The Essential Journey (2001)
The Essential Journey Deluxe 3.0 (2008)
Release date: 16 October 2001 and 26 August 2008
2001 release Certified 2x Platinum
Tracklisting:
The 2001 Release: 'Only The Young', 'Don't Stop Believin'', 'Wheel In The Sky', 'Faithfully', 'Any Way You Want It', 'Ask The Lonely', 'Who's Crying Now', 'Separate Ways (Worlds Apart)', 'Lights', 'Lovin', Touchin', Squeezin'', 'Open Arms', 'Girl Can't Help It', 'Send Her My Love', 'When You Love A Woman', 'I'll Be Alright Without You', 'After The Fall', 'Chain Reaction', 'Message Of Love', 'Somethin' To Hide', 'Line Of Fire', 'Anytime', 'Stone In Love', 'Patiently', 'Good Morning Girl', 'The Eyes Of A Woman', 'Be Good To Yourself', 'Still They Ride', 'Baby, I'm A Leavin' You', 'Mother, Father', 'Just The Same Way', 'Escape', 'The Party's Over (Hopelessly In Love)'

The 2008 Release: 'Don't Stop Believin' (Live)', 'Stone In Love (Live)', 'When I Think Of You', 'Suzanne', 'Walks Like A Lady', 'Feeling That Way', 'Mother, Father (Live)', 'I Can See It In Your Eyes'

In October 2001, a mere six months after *Arrival* hit the US market, Columbia released a two-disc set of 32 'essential' songs. Every song is from the Steve Perry era and nothing is included from the first three albums, *Dream, After Dream* or *Arrival*. Of the 32 songs, two each are from *Evolution*, Departure and *Captured*. There are three from *Trial By Fire*, four from *Raised On Radio* and five each from *Infinity* and *Frontiers*. Seven songs came from *Escape*. The remaining two, 'Only The Young' and 'Ask The Lonely' are from their respective movie soundtracks.

Given that the label dropped Journey on weak sales of *Arrival,* Columbia wanted to generate income from a valuable back catalog, hopefully riding on the buzz from the new album. As if to confirm that belief, Columbia re-released the compilation in 2008 as a *Deluxe 3.0* edition about two months after *Revelation* hit Wal-Mart's shelves. Taking advantage of the announcement of the new album with new lead singer Arnel Pineda, this new version added a short third disc that featured three tracks from the 2005 release *Live In Houston 1981: The Escape Tour*, two from *Trial By Fire,* and one each from *Raised On Radio*, *Departure* and *Infinity*.

These 40 songs do provide a satisfying overview of the Steve Perry era, but this compilation is not a necessary addition to your collection.

Greatest Hits 1978-1997 (DVD, 2003)
Produced by Steve Perry, John Kalodner and Michael Rubinstein.
Release date: 25 November 2003
DVD 4x Platinum Certified
Running time: 1:13:48
Tracklisting: 'Don't Stop Believin'', 'Wheel In The Sky', 'Faithfully', 'Any Way You

Want It', 'Separate Ways (Worlds Apart)', 'Lights', 'Lovin', Touchin', Squeezin", 'Be Good To Yourself', 'When You Love A Woman', 'Who's Crying Now', 'Send Her My Love', 'Girl Can't Help It', 'Open Arms', 'Just The Same Way', 'Stone In Love', 'Feeling That Way', 'After The Fall', 'I'll Be Alright Without You'

Not one to let back-catalog content go to waste, Columbia Music Video compiled this collection of live concert footage and music videos. Included are 18 tracks of vintage Journey from *Infinity* to *Trial By Fire*. The live tracks are superb, with five from the *Escape* tour, also available on *Live In Houston 1981 – The Escape Tour* (see below), and three from the *Raised On Radio* tour, where you can watch Mike Baird on drums and see the definitive 1980s clothing and hair stylings of bassist Randy Jackson. Another reason to watch this collection is to see Gregg Rolie and Aynsley Dunbar do their thing. Be sure to look for the Budweiser can on Rolie's Hammond organ in one video. The band did have a short-term Bud sponsorship deal at the time. Maybe, though, the most important reason to have this DVD in your video library is the *Frontiers* music videos, with 'Separate Ways (Worlds Apart)' taking center stage. This DVD is an entertaining document of Journey's peak – I can't recommend it enough.

Greatest Hits 2 (2011)
Mastered by Robert Hadley and Steve Perry
Release Date: 1 November 2011
Highest chart position: USA: 93
Running time: 1:04:07
Tracklisting: 'Stone In Love', 'After The Fall', 'Chain Reaction', 'The Party's Over (Hopelessly In Love)', 'Escape', 'Still They Ride', 'Good Morning Girl', 'Stay Awhile', 'Suzanne', 'Feeling That Way', 'Anytime', 'Walks Like A Lady', 'Little Girl', 'Just The Same Way', 'Patiently', 'When I Think Of You', 'Mother, Father (Live)'
Journey released *Eclipse* in the spring of 2011, so following an established pattern by now, Sony/Columbia took full advantage of the buzz of a new album and tour by releasing a second greatest hits album in the fall of the same year (in time for the holiday season). Around the same time, they also released a new vinyl version of the original *Greatest Hits*. This second volume includes something from every Perry era release, including 'Little Girl' from *Dream, After Dream* and a live version of 'Mother, Father' from the *Live In Houston* album. Fortunately, the album sequence didn't break tradition by putting anything between 'Feeling That Way' and 'Anytime'.

The packaging is like the original greatest hits, though primarily blue instead of red. This record was superfluous when it came out, thanks to *The Essential Journey* package. This is for collectors only. *Greatest Hits 2* hit the *Billboard* album chart for one week, peaking at number 93. It would be over a decade before Journey had another charting album.

Live Albums

Greatest Hits Live (1998)
Personnel:
Steve Perry: lead vocals
Neal Schon: lead guitar, vocals
Jonathan Cain: keyboards, vocals
Ross Valory: bass, vocals
Steve Smith: drums
Produced and mixed by Kevin Shirley at Avatar Studios, New York City
Live recordings by Kevin Elson
Additional recording: 6 May 1983, Budokan, Tokyo, Mr. Honma; 5 and 6 November 1981, Houston, Texas, Guy Charbonneau; 19 July 1983, Norman, Oklahoma, Biff Dawes
Release date: 24 March 1998
Highest chart position: USA: 79, Platinum Certified
Tracklisting: 'Don't Stop Believin'', 'Separate Ways (Worlds Apart)', 'After The Fall', 'Lovin', Touchin', Squeezin'', 'Faithfully', 'Who's Cryin' Now', 'Any Way You Want It', 'Lights', 'Stay Awhile', 'Open Arms', 'Send Her My Love', 'Still They Ride', 'Stone In Love', 'Escape', 'Line Of Fire', 'Wheel In The Sky'

These tracks are from archives of shows from 1981 to 1983. John Naatjes, an archivist and product research analyst for Sony, is given a thank you for his work in finding and recovering the tapes in 1997. As per the liner notes, these tapes had to be oven-baked to allow them to be transferred to digital tape. This was the first of the catalog-mining releases from Columbia (owned by Sony) when it realized that Journey with Steve Perry might never release another album. This and future releases would turn out to be smart business moves.

Greatest Hits Live hit the charts at its peak, number 79, in April 1998 and spent seven weeks on the *Billboard* Hot 200.

Journey 2001 (DVD, 2001)
Personnel:
Neal Schon: guitar
Ross Valory: bass
Jonathan Cain: keyboards
Steve Augeri: lead vocals
Deen Castronovo: drums
Audio produced and mixed by Kevin Shirley
Video produced by Bob Brigham, Pat Morrow and Paul Becher
Video directed by Dave Neugebauer, Kate Ferris and Josh Adams
Recorded in December 2000 in Las Vegas, Nevada
Release date: 18 December 2001
DVD Platinum Certified
Running time: 1:46:17

Tracklisting: 'Separate Ways (Worlds Apart)', 'Ask The Lonely', 'Guitar Solo', 'Stone In Love', 'Higher Place', 'Send Her My Love', 'Lights', 'Who's Crying Now', 'Piano Solo', 'Open Arms', 'Fillmore Boogie', 'All The Way', 'Escape', 'La Raza Del Sol', 'Wheel In The Sky', 'Be Good To Yourself', 'Any Way You Want It', 'Don't Stop Believin'', 'Lovin', Touchin', Squeezin'', 'Faithfully'

If you're curious about what a concert fronted by Steve Augeri looks like, then this DVD is your official opportunity to find out. You can find other streaming videos of various Augeri appearances, but the full concert experience is here. Augeri sings well, but he doesn't quite have the same energy levels as Steve Perry or Arnel Pineda. I got the sense that he was still feeling like a special guest instead of the leader.

The band, including Augeri, are as fine as ever. Without Perry, they play at much smaller venues, using a single video screen behind the stage. The mix is excellent, sounding better than *Arrival*. The setlist has only two songs from that album: 'Higher Place' and 'All The Way'. One new song made its debut.

'Fillmore Boogie' (not listed, but likely Schon) 4:47
Schon introduces this song by letting the audience know they will be in a concert video, and he asks them to show their enthusiasm. Crowd shots during this track show a few attendees dancing but plenty of empty seats as people see the opportunity to grab a drink or take a restroom break. Castronovo (wearing a sweatshirt) sets things in motion. Cain plays rhythm guitar, and Valory's competent bass can be heard in this excellent mix. 'Fillmore Boogie' is a Schon instrumental. This guitar boogie is an extended jam that harks back to the early days of the Bay Area music scene. A few bars sound melodic, evoking a bit of Steam's 'Na Na Hey Hey Kiss Him Goodbye'. Primarily a Schon workout, it's worth a listen as part of the concert experience, but it won't make anyone's list of the best rock instrumentals.

Live In Houston 1981 – The Escape Tour (CD, DVD 2005)
Personnel:
Steve Perry: lead vocals
Neal Schon: lead guitar, vocals
Jonathan Cain: keyboards, vocals
Ross Valory: bass, vocals
Steve Smith: drums
Recorded on 6 November 1981 at The Summit in Houston, Texas
Produced by Steve Perry
Mixed by Allen Sides at Ocean Way Studios, Hollywood, California
Live audio recording by Kevin Elson
Release date: 15 November 2005
DVD Platinum Certified
Running time: 1:16:57
Tracklisting: 'Escape', 'Line Of Fire', 'Lights', 'Stay Awhile', 'Open Arms'*, 'Mother,

Father', 'Jonathan Cain Solo', 'Who's Cryin' Now'*, 'Where Were You', 'Steve Smith Solo', 'Dead Or Alive', 'Don't Stop Believin''*, 'Stone In Love'*, 'Keep On Runnin'', 'Neal Schon Solo', 'Wheel In The Sky', 'Lovin', Touchin', Squeezin'', 'Any Way You Want It'*, 'The Party's Over (Hopelessly In Love)'**

* These five tracks are included as videos on Greatest Hits 1978-1997 (2003).

**available only on the CD release

Two and half months after *Generations* was first handed out to Journey concert attendees, Columbia Records were at it again. After *Arrival* hit the stores, Columbia released the comprehensive greatest hits of the Steve Perry era with *The Essential Journey*. Now, they brought in Steve Perry to produce the album and DVD of their iconic concert from the *Escape* tour in Houston, Texas. That concert aired on MTV, then the fresh, young music video channel on cable.

The CD included a live version of 'The Party's Over (Hopelessly In Love)'. Five of the 19 tracks were included in the 2003 video release of *Greatest Hits 1978-1997*.

The concert comes from when the band were at the height of their powers. It is an influential part of the pop-rock landscape of the early 1980s. Watching this concert solidified why Perry is so beloved. His voice makes average songs good, good songs great and great songs become cultural icons.

While there are no bad tracks on this live album, they only stretch out beyond the original recordings a few times. The best is a rollicking extended version of 'Wheel In The Sky'. Though it does not surpass the studio version from *Captured*, it is fun to hear the band live as they rip through 'The Party's Over (Hopelessly In Love)' on the bonus track.

The DVD includes an interview with the band and a television promo for *Escape*.

Revelation (DVD, 2008)

Personnel:
Neal Schon: all guitars, backing vocals
Jonathan Cain: keyboards, backing vocals (rhythm guitar on 'Never Walk Away')
Ross Valory: bass, backing vocals
Deen Castronovo: drums, percussion, backing vocals (lead vocal on 'Mother, Father')
Arnel Pineda: lead vocals
Produced by Kevin Shirley
Filmed at the Theatre of the Performing Arts at Planet Hollywood, Las Vegas, Nevada
Released with the Revelation album.
Running time: 1:03:01
Tracklisting: 'Sky Light', 'Any Way You Want It', 'Wheel In The Sky', 'Lights', 'After All These Years', 'Never Walk Away', 'Open Arms Prelude', 'Open Arms', 'Mother, Father', 'Wildest Dreams', 'Separate Ways (Worlds Apart)', 'Faithfully', 'Don't Stop

Believin", 'Be Good To Yourself'
Included in some three-disc packages of *Revelation*, this serves as a great introduction to Journey's new lead singer. They perform three songs from the new album. Deen Castronovo stands in for Pineda for concert favorite 'Mother, Father'. This was Pineda's third show, and his first in the United States, after his first two concerts in Chile.

'Sky Light' (Schon) 1:51
This concert-opening guitar solo from Schon can only be found on the *Revelation* concert DVD. It's mostly Schon improvising to warm up the crowd before the band segue into 'Any Way You Want It'. There are no pyrotechnics or memorable riffs.

Live In Manila (CD, DVD, BD 2009)
Personnel:
Deen Castronovo: drums, percussion
Jonathan Cain: keyboards
Arnel Pineda: lead vocals
Neal Schon: guitars
Ross Valory: bass
Audio produced by Kevin Shirley
Audio recorded by James McCullagh
Film directed and edited by Eli Tishberg
Recorded on 14 March 2009 at the Mall of Asia, Manila, Philippines
Release date: 2 October 2009
Running time: 2:22:00
Tracklisting: 'The Journey – Majestic', 'Never Walk Away', 'Only The Young', 'Ask The Lonely', 'Stone In Love', 'Keep On Runnin", 'After All These Years', 'Change For The Better', 'Wheel In The Sky', 'Lights', 'Still They Ride', 'Open Arms', 'Mother, Father', 'Wildest Dream', 'When You Love A Woman', 'Separate Ways', 'What I Needed', 'Edge Of The Blade', 'Where Did I Lose Your Love', 'Escape', 'Faithfully', 'Don't Stop Believin", 'Any Way You Want It', 'Lovin', Touchin', Squeezin", 'Turn Down The World Tonight', 'Be Good To Yourself'
While this isn't *Live In Houston 1981 – The Escape Tour*, it is a fantastic concert video. It only lacks a track or two from the first three pre-Perry albums to fit in with Schon's dream of playing the entire catalog in one long show. Despite missing those songs, this is a fine mix of the hits, the album-cut rockers, and a few new songs. What made this a truly special concert was Arnel Pineda's homecoming. He returned to the Philippines and sang in front of nearly 30,000 people at Manila's Mall of Asia.

The concert was released on Blu-Ray, DVD and CD. The packaging features a classic winged scarab design. The interior includes superb photos and liner notes by Phil Gallo.

Live In Japan 2017 (CD, DVD, BD 2019)
Personnel:
Neal Schon: lead guitar, backing vocals
Ross Valory: bass guitar, backing vocals
Jonathan Cain: keyboards, rhythm guitar, backing vocals
Steve Smith: drums
Arnel Pineda: lead vocals
Travis Thibodaux: keyboards, lead and backing vocals
Directed by Muneyuki Nowara
Recorded on 7 February 2017 at the Budokan, Tokyo, Japan
Released on 29 March 2019
Tracklisting: 'Don't Stop Believin' Intro', 'Don't Stop Believin'', 'Stone In Love', 'Who's Crying Now', 'Keep On Runnin'', 'Still They Ride', 'Escape', 'Lay It Down', 'Dead Or Alive', 'Schon Guitar Solo', 'Mother, Father', 'Cain Piano Solo', 'Open Arms', 'Separate Ways Intro', 'Separate Ways (Worlds Apart)', 'Send Her My Love', 'Chain Reaction', 'After The Fall', 'Faithfully', 'Edge Of The Blade', 'Smith Drum Solo', 'Back Talk', 'Frontiers', 'Rubicon', 'La Raza Del Sol', 'Lovin', Touchin', Squeezin''

It was a couple of months before the Hall of Fame induction, in February, that Journey performed a special concert in Japan. They played *Escape* in its entirety, took a break, came back and played all of *Frontiers*. Many of these songs hadn't been heard live for decades and, in a few cases, never made any setlists.

Each album begins with an instrumental 'introduction' not found on the studio recordings. For *Escape*, it is about a 50-second simple buildup, serving as a short intro to 'Don't Stop Believin''. It works to prepare the crowd for those well-known opening notes. After the intermission, they perform a longer (2:14) introduction, featuring plenty of classic Schon fireworks, for 'Separate Ways'.

The sound recording isn't their best, but the video looks great. The set is adequate, but this is not the most enthusiastic audience, and at times, especially with the deeper tracks, the energy flags a bit. The second keyboardist and backing vocalist is Travis Thibodaux, who is wedged behind Cain's keyboard structure and to the left of Smith's massive kit. Thibodaux does a fine job on lead vocals, taking the mic from Pineda for two songs: *Escape*'s 'Lay It Down' and *Frontiers*' 'After The Fall'.

The band add some extra music in between songs, mostly Schon, which keeps this from being a simple recital. But the best moments come after 'Rubicon', the last track on *Frontiers*. After the customary wait for the encore, Journey – freed from emulating their albums for the last 100 minutes – came out and gave an inspired performance of two songs: 'La Raza Del Sol' and 'Lovin', Touchin', Squeezin''.

'La Raza Del Sol (Live)' (Perry, Cain) 13:00
The first two and a half minutes are Journey performing a quality live version of this Perry and Cain tune. The gloves come off at that point, and the Cain-

Schon-Smith show begins as the band channel their progressive chops into a ten-minute jam, alternating between keyboards, guitar and drums. They only return to the halting theme of 'La Raza Del Sol' once in order to segue into the next jam.

Aside from an early momentary stumble by Cain, they sound formidable, playing with passion and joyful abandon. Smith's drumming is a key ingredient in the Journey sound, and it's great to hear him on this track (and the entire show). Schon, in his element, doesn't give over to unnecessary technical flash. Journey can be more than just radio-friendly hits or bland guitar rock, and this is a definitive statement. It's too bad that Smith would be out again within a year of this concert's release.

'Loving', Touchin', Squeezin" (Perry) 10:44
They roll into the second encore directly from the first, turning a long three-and-a-half-minute intro into a blues jam, like a pumped-up 'Rocky Mountain Way'. Schon leads the crowd in some modest call-and-response with the guitar. The audience know this song better than 'La Raza Del Sol', so when the band drop down into those opening bars, the cheers threaten to drown out Pineda singing the opening line, 'You make me weak'. After playing the main song for a couple of minutes, the band dive into blues jam mode, with Cain and Schon trading riffs. It's an entertaining three and a half minutes.

Toward the end of this section, Pineda encourages the crowd to get ready for the iconic 'na na na na' part. They do a decent job with it, and at 9:33, the band halt, like the studio cut, allowing the unaccompanied vocals to sustain for a few seconds. The final minutes wrap up the song and the concert. These encores are high energy and show what Journey can do when unconstrained.

Live From Lollapalooza (2022)
Personnel:
Credited as the Lollapalooza Band
Neal Schon: guitars, vocals
Jonathan Cain: keyboards, guitar, vocals
Arnel Pineda: lead vocals
Deen Castronovo: drums, vocals
Narada Michael Walden: drums
Jason Derlatka: keyboards, vocals
Marco Mendez: bass, vocals
Todd Jensen is in the credits, but he did not perform or appear on this recording
Produced by David Kalmusky and Journey
Recorded by David Kalmusky
Mixed by David Kalmusky at Addiction Sound Studios, Blackbird Studios and The Blue Loft, Nashville, Tennessee
Recorded on 29 July 2021 at Grant Park, Chicago, Illinois
Release date: 9 December 2022

Running time: 1:38:54

Tracklisting: 'Separate Ways', 'Only The Young', 'Guitar Interlude', 'Stone In Love', 'Be Good To Yourself', 'Just The Same Way', 'Lights', 'Still They Ride', 'Escape', 'La Do Da', 'Piano Interlude', 'Who's Crying Now', 'Guitar Interlude', 'Wheel In The Sky', 'Ask The Lonely', 'Open Arms', 'Lovin', Touchin', Squeezin'', 'Faithfully', 'Any Way You Want It', 'Don't Stop Believin''

Freedom hit online retailers and streaming services in early July 2022. This is usually a signal that Sony/Columbia is going to repackage or release something from the classic era catalog to take advantage of any buzz the new album creates. This time, it is the reissue of *Live In Houston 1981 – The Escape Tour* on double vinyl LPs. In addition to the regular black vinyl, there is a special edition featuring sides A and B on white vinyl and sides C and D on red vinyl.

Then there was the work on 'Separate Ways (Worlds Apart)' for the Netflix television series *Stranger Things*. What began as a remix for a credit sequence was lengthened with Steve Perry's help and added to the show's fourth-season soundtrack. Perry also worked with Bryce Miller, a bit less successfully, on giving the same remix treatment to 'Only The Young', which was released in the fall of 2023. (See *Frontiers*' 'Related Tracks' for all three of these remixes.)

Despite all this activity in 2022, Journey decided to release their July 2021 Lollapalooza show in time for Christmas 2022. The concert, recorded at Lollapalooza in Chicago, featured an unusual Journey lineup. Both Narada Michael Walden and Deen Castronovo take their respective thrones behind their drum kits. On bass, Marco Mendoza makes his first and only appearance on an official Journey record, though we will meet him again on the next unofficial Journey album. Mendoza had worked with Schon in the past and he was tapped to replace Randy Jackson, who had to have back surgery. For some reason, Todd Jensen, Journey's current bassist, is credited, though he does not appear in the concert. We see Jason Derlatka on keyboards and backing vocals for the first time on video. He had been part of the touring band and provided backing vocals to six songs on *Freedom*.

Pineda provides all the lead vocals except for 'Just The Same Way', where Cain sings Rolie's part. Everyone sounds solid. Schon's solo takes less than a minute, which is a slight disappointment. By contrast, Cain's keyboard solo goes on for three minutes. The crowd get very little screen time. Most of the cameras are trained on individual band members, and the cuts are many and varied. The highest point of the show is the final song, 'Don't Stop Believin'', where the crowd don't wait for any encouragement from Pineda. They belt out the verses – it's a high-energy moment.

The 20-track double CD was released on Frontiers Records. The package includes two audio CDs and a single DVD. Band photos from the show are sprinkled throughout the digipak. Jim Welch is once again responsible for the art direction. The scarab, if it can be called that, is more abstract than ever. The wings are mere outlines with a tie-dyed color scheme.

The album is an unnecessary addition to the catalog, but it's still fun to watch. This is identical to their usual tour experience except for the two drummers. There is no risk-taking here, as nothing from after *Raised On Radio* is included. That said, if you want to know what to expect from a 2020 Journey concert experience, this set is a great choice.

Neal Schon – Journey Through Time (2023)
Personnel:
Neal Schon: guitars, vocals
Deen Castronovo: drums, lead and backing vocals
Marco Mendoza: bass guitar, vocals
John Varn: keyboards, vocals
Gregg Rolie: keyboards, lead and backing vocals
Produced and mixed by Neal Schon and Jim Reitzel
Recorded by Adam Canby
Film produced by Adam Reader
Film directed by Kris Schooler
Recorded on 9 February 2018 at The Independent in San Francisco, California
Release date: 19 May 2023
Running time: 2:41:52
Tracklisting: 'I'm Gonna Leave You', 'Look Into The Future', 'Kohoutek', 'Daydream', 'La Do Da', 'Line Of Fire', 'Walks Like A Lady', 'Feelin' That Way', 'Anytime', 'Lights', 'Still They Ride', 'Separate Ways', 'Lovin', Touchin', Squeezin'', 'Medley: Patiently, Trial By Fire, And Stay Awhile', 'Mystery Mountain', 'Of A Lifetime', 'Just The Same Way', 'Lovin' You Is Easy', 'Lady Luck', 'You're On Your Own', 'Hustler', 'Nickle And Dime' (Sic), 'People', 'Mother, Father', 'Any Way You Want It', 'Don't Stop Believin'', 'Black Magic Woman', 'Oye Como Va'.

While not an official Journey release, this three-disc set (along with the complete show on a single DVD) officially falls under Neal Schon's individual output. However, except for the two Santana songs at the end of the set, every track is part of the Journey catalog. And 'Journey' is in the title. Schon has made no secret about his desire to tour without an opening act that would have two 90-minute sets that dig deep into the catalog. This is as close as he has come to achieving this vision.

Happily, Gregg Rolie is part of this band. It's good to see him sitting behind that Hammond B3 cabinet. His voice isn't as strong as it once was, but he does decent work here, especially on 'Look Into The Future' and 'You're On Your Own'. Deen Castronovo fills the shoes of Steve Perry and Arnel Pineda with clear ease. Playing drums while singing lead is never a simple task, and he does commendable work. He steps out from behind the kit for a guitar and vocalist medley of 'Patiently', 'Trial By Fire' and 'Stay Awhile'. The only disappointment during the set was 'Don't Stop Believin'', which lacked energy, but as the 27th song, maybe band and audience fatigue was setting in. Marco Mendoza sings lead vocals on 'Hustler' and introduces 'Oye Como Va' in Spanish. Note that 'Nickel And Dime' is misspelled on the package, as noted above.

The video quality and camera angles suggest a lower budget than the Lollapalooza concert. While the sound quality is not great, this is still a wonderful experience. Where the Lollapalooza concert doesn't add much to the repertoire, here we have quite a bit of Journey's early catalog performed live. It is a great trip through the full past of Journey. Adding the Santana tunes at the end is a good reminder of where Rolie and Schon originated.

Unfortunately, for the continued viability of this project, Schon didn't work out the legalities of using the Journey name to Rolie's satisfaction. Rolie stated that Schon had not obtained the rights to the songs issued on this album and the DVD. He also pointed out that advertising for European shows, where Journey had not toured for more than 15 years, was deceptive, featuring 'Journey' in a larger font than 'Through Time'. Rolie did not want fans to be disappointed, and he wanted no part of the potential reputational damage this would cause.

Jim Welch handles the art direction again, and at this point, we can safely blame him and Schon for this atrocious 'winged eyeball in the heart over a glowing pyramid' cartoon art that graces the Digipak cover. Despite the ugly packaging, this is a set worth owning for Journey fans. It's a fine, if amateurish, video production that provides a couple of hours of solid entertainment. Seeing Gregg Rolie behind the Hammond B3 again is worth the price.

Selected Films

Frontiers And Beyond Tour Documentary (1984)
An odd duck of a tour film, this was produced by NFL Films, complete with voiceover narration from the great John Facenda. A lot of the film covers the crew and what it takes to keep a massive tour moving across the land. To that end, it's a great behind-the-scenes look at the *Frontiers* tour at the height of Journey's popularity.

There are other tour documentaries, but this is the best that goes beyond concert footage and the usual promotional copy. Check out the *Raised On Radio Tour* for another example.

Don't Stop Believin': Every Man's Journey (2013)
Ramona S. Diaz directs this documentary about Arnel Pineda becoming the new lead singer. The film serves as an excellent introduction to this singer from Manila. The band are given a few minutes to present their history, but the primary subject is Pineda. Seeing the fan reaction, watching Pineda shine in his new role and seeing the aging, cantankerous crew of musicians he has joined – at times condescending and at other times supportive and encouraging – is fascinating for fans. Pineda, by all accounts, is a humble man with prodigious talent, which means he's a perfect fit in a band full of big egos, each with their enormous talent. This is highly recommended for those who want to know more about Arnel Pineda. The film closes on a high note with a video for 'City Of Hope'.

Bibliography

Bias, K., *Journey – A 50th Anniversary Celebration* (a360 Media, New York City, 2023).
Cain, J., *Don't Stop Believin': The Man, The Band, And The Song That Inspired Generations* (Zondervan, Grand Rapids, 2018).
Daniels, N., *Don't Stop Believin': The Untold Story Of Journey* (Omnibus Press, London, 2011).
DeRiso, N., *Journey: Worlds Apart* (Time Passages, Lakeshore, Maryland, 2023).
Golland, D.H., *Livin' Just To Find Emotion: Journey And The Story Of American Rock* (Rowman and Littlefield, Lanham, 2024).
Griffith, M. (ed.), *Modern Drummer Legends: Steve Smith* (Modern Drummer Media, Boca Raton, 2022).
Jackson, B., *The Art Of Stanley Mouse: California Dreams* (Soft Skull Press, New York, 2015).
Mouse, S., *Freehand: The Art Of Stanley Mouse* (SLG Books, Berkeley, 1993).
Santana, C., *The Universal Tone: Bringing My Story To Light* (Little, Brown and Company, New York, 2014).
Selvin, J., *Summer Of Love: The Inside Story Of LSD, Rock & Roll, And Free Love, And High Times In The Wild West* (Dutton, Boston, 1994).

Websites
www.journeymusic.com (Official band site)
www.journey-zone.com (Fan site)
www.fortheloveofsteveperry.com (Fan site)
www.ronsouth.blogspot.com (Fan site)
www.billboard.com (USA Chart history)

Band Member Sites
www.greggrolie.com
www.steveperry.com
www.jonathancain.org
www.arnelpineda.com
www.vitalinformation.com (Steve Smith)
www.aynsleydunbar.com
www.steveaugeri.com
www.schonmusic.com (Neal Schon)
www.jasonderlatka.com

Also available from Sonicbond

Allman Brothers Band – on track
Every album, every song

Every album, every song
Andrew Wild
Paperback
128 pages
46 colour photographs
978-1-78952-252-5
£15.99
$22.95

Every album and every song by this legendary American band.

In 1973, the Allman Brothers Band were one of the most popular in America. They headlined the Watkins Glen Summer Jam – attended by 600,000 people – and their album *Brothers and Sisters* was number one for five weeks. The group made the cover of *Newsweek* and *Rolling Stone* named them 'band of the year'.

Always a strong live draw, in the two years prior to Watkins Glen, they released one of the greatest live albums of all time and lost two founding members in motorcycle accidents, including guitar genius Duane Allman. Drug use and a ruinous 1976 court case forced the band apart, but a three-album reunion between 1978 and 1982 rekindled some of the old fire. It was with their twentieth anniversary and second reformation in 1989 that provided a degree of stability.

Their legacy of eleven studio albums and six contemporaneous live albums include classics such as their self-titled debut, the sophomore *Idlewild South*, the definitive live document *At Fillmore East* and the astounding final album *Hittin' The Note* from 2003.

The music of the Allman Brothers is the pure distillation of the four main ingredients of American music: blues, rock, jazz and country. At their best, they transcended genre: they just were.

Also available from Sonicbond

Van Halen *revised edition*
Every album, every song

Morgan Brown
Paperback
144 pages
37 colour photographs
978-1-78952-256-4
£15.99
$22.95

Every album and every song by this hugely successful American heavy rock band.

Van Halen are arguably America's greatest-ever rock n' roll band. From inauspicious roots as a backyard covers outfit, they went on to revolutionise and revitalise heavy rock, creating a world-conquering blend of heavy metal power, punk energy and pop hooks. Armed with staggering musical virtuosity and irresistible charisma, they sold millions of records and spawned legions of imitators. From their humble origins and meteoric rise, through some dark, troubled years, to their triumphant rebirth, the band produced a remarkable body of work.

In this thorough and illuminating book, Morgan Brown guides us song by song through the band's classic albums, charting their development from Sunset Strip upstarts to multi-platinum stadium rockers and beyond. We'll examine the music's ingredients and inspirations and meet the characters behind the songs, including visionary guitar genius the late Edward Van Halen, motormouth master showman David Lee Roth, and his replacement, powerful vocalist Sammy Hagar, who ushered in a new era for the band. Equally suitable for inquisitive new listeners or long-time fans, this book is both an in-depth guide to and an enthusiastic celebration of the career of a truly legendary band. Feel like diving in? Well, as Roth said, go ahead and jump!

Also available from Sonicbond

REO Speedwagon – on track
Every album, every song

Jim Romag
Paperback
144 pages
47 colour photographs
978-1-78952-262-4
£15.99
$22.95

Every album by the hugely successful US AOR band.

Once, there were four university students who started a rock band named after a firetruck. Five and a half decades later, REO Speedwagon are still going strong, still drawing massive crowds, and, thankfully, have no plans to stop. With classic albums like the multi-platinum *You Can Tune A Piano, But You Can't Tuna Fish* and the ten million-selling *Hi Infidelity*, REO conquered America's heartland, then the nation, and finally – as a ten-year 'overnight sensation' – the world. It was the rock tunes like 'Golden Country' and 'Back on the Road Again' that built their reputation before the ballads like 'Keep on Loving You' and 'Can't Fight this Feeling' brought them global fame. REO have sold over 40 million records under their own name and are featured on the soundtracks to scores of films and television programs, including *Supernatural* and *Ozark*.

REO Speedwagon On Track shines a light on the band's lengthy career. This book delves into the tracks on each of their 16 studio albums, their official live releases, and several compilations, while also providing a glimpse of some of the band members' outside projects, creating a comprehensive companion to the music of this American institution.

Also available from Sonicbond

Deep Purple From 1984
Every album, every song

Phil Kafcaloudes
Paperback
160 pages
43 colour photographs
978-1-78952-354-6
£16.99
$22.95

Every album in the second part of the career of this world-famous British rock institution.

In 2024, Deep Purple celebrated the fortieth anniversary of their reunion by releasing their 23rd album, =1. Some band members thought the 1984 reunion would fizzle out after one album, but it flourished despite internecine strife, illness and the loss of two founders in Richie Blackmore and Jon Lord. As other members approached eighty years of age, they still succeeded in producing albums that were to be among their most successful.

This book tells this sometimes bizarre post-reunion story through their music and, to an extent, their touring. Neither was always completely successful, as the band seemed to be either searching for synergy in their sound or for a commercial product that did not sacrifice artistic integrity. The lyrics are especially valuable because they reveal the hardship of the road and insights into their own growing frustrations with society. In doing this, the band has not just resurfaced but written a new story for a new audience.

All these things make this phase of Deep Purple an interesting study, not just of a band loved by so many but also of musicians who just wanted to play their music and sometimes found that it was not quite as simple as that.

Also available from Sonicbond

On Track series

AC/DC – Chris Sutton 978-1-78952-307-2
Allman Brothers Band – Andrew Wild 978-1-78952-252-5
Tori Amos – Lisa Torem 978-1-78952-142-9
Aphex Twin – Beau Waddell 978-1-78952-267-9
Asia – Peter Braidis 978-1-78952-099-6
Badfinger – Robert Day-Webb 978-1-878952-176-4
Barclay James Harvest – Keith and Monica Domone 978-1-78952-067-5
Beck – Arthur Lizie 978-1-78952-258-7
The Beat, General Public, Fine Young Cannibals – Steve Parry 978-1-78952-274-7
The Beatles 1962-1996 – Alberto Bravin and Andrew Wild 978-1-78952-355-3
The Beatles Solo 1969-1980 – Andrew Wild 978-1-78952-030-9
Blue Oyster Cult – Jacob Holm-Lupo 978-1-78952-007-1
Blur – Matt Bishop 978-178952-164-1
Marc Bolan and T.Rex – Peter Gallagher 978-1-78952-124-5
David Bowie 1964 to 1982 – Carl Ewens 978-1-78952-324-9
David Bowie 1963 to 2016 – Don Klees 978-1-78952-351-5
Kate Bush – Bill Thomas 978-1-78952-097-2
The Byrds – Andy McArthur 978-1-78952-280-8
Camel – Hamish Kuzminski 978-1-78952-040-8
Captain Beefheart – Opher Goodwin 978-1-78952-235-8
Caravan – Andy Boot 978-1-78952-127-6
Cardiacs – Eric Benac 978-1-78952-131-3
Wendy Carlos – Mark Marrington 978-1-78952-331-7
The Carpenters – Paul Tornbohm 978-1-78952-301-0
Nick Cave and The Bad Seeds – Dominic Sanderson 978-1-78952-240-2
Eric Clapton Solo – Andrew Wild 978-1-78952-141-2
The Clash (revised edition) – Nick Assirati 978-1-78952-325-6
Elvis Costello and The Attractions – Georg Purvis 978-1-78952-129-0
Crosby, Stills and Nash – Andrew Wild 978-1-78952-039-2
Creedence Clearwater Revival – Tony Thompson 978-1-78952-237-2
Crowded House – Jon Magidsohn 978-1-78952-292-1
The Damned – Morgan Brown 978-1-78952-136-8
David Bowie 1964 to 1982 – Carl Ewens 978-1-78952-324-9
David Bowie 1964 to 1982 – Carl Ewens 978-1-78952-324-9
Deep Purple and Rainbow 1968-79 – Steve Pilkington 978-1-78952-002-6
Deep Purple from 1984 – Phil Kafcaloudes 978-1-78952-354-6
Depeche Mode – Brian J. Robb 978-1-78952-277-8
Dire Straits – Andrew Wild 978-1-78952-044-6
The Divine Comedy – Alan Draper 978-1-78952-308-9
The Doors – Tony Thompson 978-1-78952-137-5
Dream Theater – Jordan Blum 978-1-78952-050-7

Bob Dylan 1962-1970 – Opher Goodwin 978-1-78952-275-2
Eagles – John Van der Kiste 978-1-78952-260-0
Earth, Wind and Fire – Bud Wilkins 978-1-78952-272-3
Electric Light Orchestra – Barry Delve 978-1-78952-152-8
Emerson Lake and Palmer – Mike Goode 978-1-78952-000-2
Fairport Convention – Kevan Furbank 978-1-78952-051-4
Peter Gabriel – Graeme Scarfe 978-1-78952-138-2
Genesis – Stuart MacFarlane 978-1-78952-005-7
Gentle Giant – Gary Steel 978-1-78952-058-3
Gong – Kevan Furbank 978-1-78952-082-8
Green Day – William E. Spevack 978-1-78952-261-7
Steve Hackett – Geoffrey Feakes 978-1-78952-098-9
Hall and Oates – Ian Abrahams 978-1-78952-167-2
Peter Hammill – Richard Rees Jones 978-1-78952-163-4
Roy Harper – Opher Goodwin 978-1-78952-130-6
Hawkwind (new edition) – Duncan Harris 978-1-78952-290-7
Jimi Hendrix – Emma Stott 978-1-78952-175-7
The Hollies – Andrew Darlington 978-1-78952-159-7
Horslips – Richard James 978-1-78952-263-1
The Human League and The Sheffield Scene – Andrew Darlington 978-1-78952-186-3
Humble Pie –Robert Day-Webb 978-1-78952-2761
Ian Hunter – G. Mick Smith 978-1-78952-304-1
The Incredible String Band – Tim Moon 978-1-78952-107-8
INXS – Manny Grillo 978-1-78952-302-7
Iron Maiden – Steve Pilkington 978-1-78952-061-3
Joe Jackson – Richard James 978-1-78952-189-4
The Jam – Stan Jeffries 978-1-78952-299-0
Jefferson Airplane – Richard Butterworth 978-1-78952-143-6
Jethro Tull – Jordan Blum 978-1-78952-016-3
J. Geils Band – James Romag 978-1-78952-332-4
Elton John in the 1970s – Peter Kearns 978-1-78952-034-7
Billy Joel – Lisa Torem 978-1-78952-183-2
Journey – Doug Thornton 978-1-78952-337-9
Judas Priest – John Tucker 978-1-78952-018-7
Kansas – Kevin Cummings 978-1-78952-057-6
Killing Joke – Nic Ransome 978-1-78952-273-0
The Kinks – Martin Hutchinson 978-1-78952-172-6
Korn – Matt Karpe 978-1-78952-153-5
Led Zeppelin – Steve Pilkington 978-1-78952-151-1
Level 42 – Matt Philips 978-1-78952-102-3
Little Feat – Georg Purvis – 978-1-78952-168-9
Magnum – Matthew Taylor – 978-1-78952-286-0

Also available from Sonicbond

Aimee Mann – Jez Rowden 978-1-78952-036-1
Ralph McTell – Paul O. Jenkins 978-1-78952-294-5
Metallica – Barry Wood 978-1-78952-269-3
Joni Mitchell – Peter Kearns 978-1-78952-081-1
The Moody Blues – Geoffrey Feakes 978-1-78952-042-2
Motorhead – Duncan Harris 978-1-78952-173-3
Nektar – Scott Meze – 978-1-78952-257-0
New Order – Dennis Remmer – 978-1-78952-249-5
Nightwish – Simon McMurdo – 978-1-78952-270-9
Nirvana – William E. Spevack 978-1-78952-318-8
Laura Nyro – Philip Ward 978-1-78952-182-5
Oasis – Andrew Rooney 978-1-78952-300-3
Phil Ochs – Opher Goodwin 978-1-78952-326-3
Mike Oldfield – Ryan Yard 978-1-78952-060-6
Opeth – Jordan Blum 978-1-78-952-166-5
Pearl Jam – Ben L. Connor 978-1-78952-188-7
Tom Petty – Richard James 978-1-78952-128-3
Pink Floyd – Richard Butterworth 978-1-78952-242-6
The Police – Pete Braidis 978-1-78952-158-0
Porcupine Tree (Revised Edition) – Nick Holmes 978-1-78952-346-1
Procol Harum – Scott Meze 978-1-78952-315-7
Queen – Andrew Wild 978-1-78952-003-3
Radiohead – William Allen 978-1-78952-149-8
Gerry Rafferty – John Van der Kiste 978-1-78952-349-2
Rancid – Paul Matts 978-1-78952-187-0
Lou Reed 1972-1986 – Ethan Roy 978-1-78952-283-9
Renaissance – David Detmer 978-1-78952-062-0
REO Speedwagon – Jim Romag 978-1-78952-262-4
The Rolling Stones 1963-80 – Steve Pilkington 978-1-78952-017-0
Linda Ronstadt 1969-1989 – Daryl O. Lawrence 987-1-78952-293-8
Roxy Music – Michael Kulikowski 978-1-78952-335-5
Rush 1973 to 1982 – Richard James 978-1-78952-338-6
Sensational Alex Harvey Band – Peter Gallagher 978-1-7952-289-1
The Small Faces and The Faces – Andrew Darlington 978-1-78952-316-4
The Smashing Pumpkins – Matt Karpe 978-1-7952-291-4
The Smiths and Morrissey – Tommy Gunnarsson 978-1-78952-140-5
Soft Machine – Scott Meze 978-1078952-271-6
Sparks 1969-1979 – Chris Sutton 978-1-78952-279-2
Spirit – Rev. Keith A. Gordon – 978-1-78952- 248-8
Stackridge – Alan Draper 978-1-78952-232-7
Status Quo the Frantic Four Years – Richard James 978-1-78952-160-3
Steely Dan – Jez Rowden 978-1-78952-043-9

The Stranglers – Martin Hutchinson 978-1-78952-323-2
Talk Talk – Gary Steel 978-1-78952-284-6
Talking Heads – David Starkey 978-178952-353-9
Tears For Fears – Paul Clark – 978-178952-238-9
Thin Lizzy – Graeme Stroud 978-1-78952-064-4
Tool – Matt Karpe 978-1-78952-234-1
Toto – Jacob Holm-Lupo 978-1-78952-019-4
U2 – Eoghan Lyng 978-1-78952-078-1
UFO – Richard James 978-1-78952-073-6
Ultravox – Brian J. Robb 978-1-78952-330-0
Van Der Graaf Generator – Dan Coffey 978-1-78952-031-6
Van Halen – Morgan Brown – 9781-78952-256-3
Suzanne Vega – Lisa Torem 978-1-78952-281-5
Jack White And The White Stripes – Ben L. Connor 978-1-78952-303-4
The Who – Geoffrey Feakes 978-1-78952-076-7
Roy Wood and the Move – James R Turner 978-1-78952-008-8
Yes (new edition) – Stephen Lambe 978-1-78952-282-2
Neil Young 1963 to 1970 – Oper Goodwin 978-1-78952-298-3
Frank Zappa 1966 to 1979 – Eric Benac 978-1-78952-033-0
Warren Zevon – Peter Gallagher 978-1-78952-170-2
The Zombies – Emma Stott 978-1-78952-297-6
10CC – Peter Kearns 978-1-78952-054-5

Decades Series

The Bee Gees in the 1960s – Andrew Mon Hughes et al 978-1-78952-148-1
The Bee Gees in the 1970s – Andrew Mon Hughes et al 978-1-78952-179-5
Black Sabbath in the 1970s – Chris Sutton 978-1-78952-171-9
Britpop – Peter Richard Adams and Matt Pooler 978-1-78952-169-6
Phil Collins in the 1980s – Andrew Wild 978-1-78952-185-6
Alice Cooper in the 1970s – Chris Sutton 978-1-78952-104-7
Alice Cooper in the 1980s – Chris Sutton 978-1-78952-259-4
Curved Air in the 1970s – Laura Shenton 978-1-78952-069-9
Donovan in the 1960s – Jeff Fitzgerald 978-1-78952-233-4
Bob Dylan in the 1980s – Don Klees 978-1-78952-157-3
Brian Eno in the 1970s – Gary Parsons 978-1-78952-239-6
Faith No More in the 1990s – Matt Karpe 978-1-78952-250-1
Fleetwood Mac in the 1970s – Andrew Wild 978-1-78952-105-4
Fleetwood Mac in the 1980s – Don Klees 978-178952-254-9
Focus in the 1970s – Stephen Lambe 978-1-78952-079-8
Free and Bad Company in the 1970s – John Van der Kiste 978-1-78952-178-8
Genesis in the 1970s – Bill Thomas 978178952-146-7
George Harrison in the 1970s – Eoghan Lyng 978-1-78952-174-0

Also available from Sonicbond

Kiss in the 1970s – Peter Gallagher 978-1-78952-246-4
Manfred Mann's Earth Band in the 1970s – John Van der Kiste 978178952-243-3
Marillion in the 1980s – Nathaniel Webb 978-1-78952-065-1
Van Morrison in the 1970s – Peter Childs – 978-1-78952-241-9
Mott the Hoople & Ian Hunter in the 1970s – John Van der Kiste 978-1-78-952-162-7
Pink Floyd In The 1970s – Georg Purvis 978-1-78952-072-9
Suzi Quatro in the 1970s – Darren Johnson 978-1-78952-236-5
Queen in the 1970s – James Griffiths 978-1-78952-265-5
Roxy Music in the 1970s – Dave Thompson 978-1-78952-180-1
Slade in the 1970s – Darren Johnson 978-1-78952-268-6
Status Quo in the 1980s – Greg Harper 978-1-78952-244-0
Tangerine Dream in the 1970s – Stephen Palmer 978-1-78952-161-0
The Sweet in the 1970s – Darren Johnson 978-1-78952-139-9
Uriah Heep in the 1970s – Steve Pilkington 978-1-78952-103-0
Van der Graaf Generator in the 1970s – Steve Pilkington 978-1-78952-245-7
Rick Wakeman in the 1970s – Geoffrey Feakes 978-1-78952-264-8
Yes in the 1980s – Stephen Lambe with David Watkinson 978-1-78952-125-2

Rock Classics Series

90125 by Yes – Stephen Lambe 978-1-78952-329-4
Bat Out Of Hell by Meatloaf – Geoffrey Feakes 978-1-78952-320-1
Bringing It All Back Home by Bob Dylan – Opher Goodwin 978-1-78952-314-0
Californication by Red Hot Chili Peppers - Matt Karpe 978-1-78952-348-5
Crime Of The Century by Supertramp – Steve Pilkington 978-1-78952-327-0
The Dreaming by Kate Bush – Peter Kearns 978-1-78952-341-6
Let It Bleed by The Rolling Stones – John Van der Kiste 978-1-78952-309-6
Pawn Hearts by Van Der Graaf Generator – Paolo Carnelli 978-1-78952-357-7
Purple Rain by Prince – Matt Karpe 978-1-78952-322-5
The White Album by The Beatles – Opher Goodwin 978-1-78952-333-1

On Screen Series

Carry On… – Stephen Lambe 978-1-78952-004-0
David Cronenberg – Patrick Chapman 978-1-78952-071-2
Doctor Who: The David Tennant Years – Jamie Hailstone 978-1-78952-066-8
James Bond – Andrew Wild 978-1-78952-010-1
Monty Python – Steve Pilkington 978-1-78952-047-7
Seinfeld Seasons 1 to 5 – Stephen Lambe 978-1-78952-012-5

Other Books

1967: A Year In Psychedelic Rock 978-1-78952-155-9
1970: A Year In Rock – John Van der Kiste 978-1-78952-147-4
1972: The Year Progressive Rock Ruled The World – Kevan Furbank 978-1-78952-288-4
1973: The Golden Year of Progressive Rock 978-1-78952-165-8

Also available from Sonicbond

Eric Clapton Sessions – Andrew Wild 978-1-78952-177-1
Dark Horse Records – Aaron Badgley 978-1-78952-287-7
Derek Taylor: For Your Radioactive Children – Andrew Darlington 978-1-78952-038-5
Ghosts – Journeys To Post-Pop – Matthew Restall 978-1-78952-334-8
The Golden Age of Easy Listening – Derek Taylor 978-1-78952-285-3
The Golden Road: The Recording History of The Grateful Dead – John Kilbride 978-1-78952-156-6
Hoggin' The Page – Groudhogs The Classic Years – Martyn Hanson 978-1-78952-343-0
Iggy and The Stooges On Stage 1967-1974 – Per Nilsen 978-1-78952-101-6
Jon Anderson and the Warriors – the Road to Yes – David Watkinson 978-1-78952-059-0
Magic: The David Paton Story – David Paton 978-1-78952-266-2
Misty: The Music of Johnny Mathis – Jakob Baekgaard 978-1-78952-247-1
Musical Guide To Red By King Crimson – Andrew Keeling 978-1-78952-321-8
Nu Metal: A Definitive Guide – Matt Karpe 978-1-78952-063-7
Philip Lynott – Renegade – Alan Byrne 978-1-78952-339-3
Remembering Live Aid – Andrew Wild 978-1-78952-328-7
Thank You For The Days - Fans Of The Kinks Share 60 Years of Stories – Ed. Chris Kocher 978-1-78952-342-3
The Sonicbond On Track Sampler – 978-1-78952-190-0
The Sonicbond Progressive Rock Sampler (Ebook only) – 978-1-78952-056-9
Tommy Bolin: In and Out of Deep Purple – Laura Shenton 978-1-78952-070-5
Maximum Darkness – Deke Leonard 978-1-78952-048-4
The Twang Dynasty – Deke Leonard 978-1-78952-049-1

... and many more to come!

Would you like to write for Sonicbond Publishing?

We are mainly a music publisher, but we also occasionally publish in other genres including film and television. At Sonicbond Publishing we are always on the look-out for authors, particularly for our two main series, On Track and Decades.

Mixing fact with in depth analysis, the On Track series examines the entire recorded work of a particular musical artist or group. All genres are considered from easy listening and jazz to 60s soul to 90s pop, via rock and metal.

The Decades series singles out a particular decade in an artist or group's history and focuses on that decade in more detail than may be allowed in the On Track series.

While professional writing experience would, of course, be an advantage, the most important qualification is to have real enthusiasm and knowledge of your subject. First-time authors are welcomed, but the ability to write well in English is essential.

Sonicbond Publishing has distribution throughout Europe and North America, and all our books are also published in E-book form. Authors will be paid a royalty based on sales of their book. Further details about our books are available from www.sonicbondpublishing.com. To contact us, complete the contact form there or email info@sonicbondpublishing.co.uk